Life, Sex, and Ideas

Life, Sex and Ideas
The Good Life without God

A. C. Grayling

*I applied mine heart to know,
and to search, and to seek out wisdom,
and the reason of things.*
ECCLESIASTES 7:25

OXFORD
UNIVERSITY PRESS

OXFORD
UNIVERSITY PRESS

Oxford   New York
Auckland   Bangkok   Buenos Aires
Cape Town   Chennai   Dar es Salaam   Delhi   Hong Kong   Istanbul
Karachi   Kolkata   Kuala Lumpur   Madrid   Melbourne   Mexico City   Mumbai
Nairobi   São Paulo   Shanghai   Taipei   Tokyo   Toronto

First published by Oxford University Press, Inc., 2003
198 Madison Avenue, New York, New York 10016
www.oup.com

First issued as an Oxford University Press paperback, 2005

Library of Congress Cataloging-in-Publication Data is available
at the Library of Congress
ISBN 978-0-19-517755-8

Contents

Nature and Naturalness

Reading and Thinking

For Katie:

Tibi suavis daedala tellius summittit flores.

Introduction

There is no wealth but life.

RUSKIN

Of all the questions we can ask ourselves the most important is: how is one best to live? The question has components. How and where is one to find the resources to construct meaning in one's life? How shall one justify one's existence and make it worthwhile for oneself and others? How shall one make experience valuable, and keep growing and learning as one does so, by this means attaining a degree of understanding of oneself and the world?

As regards resources, some philosophers have said that the answer is: art, love and the pursuit of knowledge. Attentiveness to these, and their fruits, helps in finding the richly complex answer to the general question. In part these resources do it by promoting the powers of observation and discernment connoted in Pater's remark that 'it is only the dullness of the eye that makes any two things seem alike' – for while the eyes of the mind are dim, they see none of the satisfactions that exist in particularity, excellence, and depth; and one will therefore have little of these things to give in return.

In *The Trial* Kafka explored the traditional sources of meaning (to love and art he added, as most have done, religion – that invention of the serpent in Eden) and claimed to find them wanting. Perhaps he thereby anticipated the 'postmodern' despair over the fact that the Enlightenment, despite its philosophy and hopes for education, did not succeed in civilising the human spirit, which remains enthralled to war, injustice, rapine, superstition, intolerance and racism. But those who defend Enlightenment values reply that reality has not shattered their dream of the heavenly city to be built on earth. Instead, it strengthens it. No one is naïve enough to think that the dream can come fully true, but that is not the point. The point rather is to make it come as true as possible. It is enough of a duty and a prize for some that they feel life's worth resides precisely in fighting for that goal, trying to enlist as many as possible to join the enterprise, and to help carry the hope head-high through the dirty waters of history. What would the world, and life in the world, be like without such hope? Hopelessness in this regard is the prompt for two kinds of suicide: the literal kind, and the kind in which people slay their autonomy and rationality by trying to believe that since this world is no good, there must be a posthumous alternative where all will be better.

Is talk of 'art, love and knowledge' mere cliché, mere piety? No. If it sounds like either it is because we have long recognised the truth that they are our best resources. Saying it is like saying something as obvious yet true as that one must eat to live – and these resources feed the spirit. It is a matter of the states they induce in us, and what they make of us. They offer us nothing less than the chance to live flourishingly, richly, each pulse filled with significance, where such living spills over with return, giving something back to what prompted it. Contrast such living with boredom, suffering, impoverishment of spirit, fear, hatred – and one sees the force of Epictetus's question, when, after discussing the considered life with his pupils, he asked them: 'How long will you delay to be wise?'

A civilised society is one which never ceases having a discussion with itself about what human life should best be. Some would, with justice, say that if we want ours to be such a society we should all take part in the discussion. This book is, with appropriate diffidence, an attempt at such a contribution. It consists of short informal essays about aspects of ethics, ideas and culture. It is a miscellany, the essays having begun life as independent entities; but their arrangement is deliberate, for they group together, and occasionally link together, in ways designed to add to the topics addressed in neighbouring essays. But they are a miscellany nonetheless; and each asks no more than to be read on its own.

The essays are mostly brief and suggestive rather than long and discursive, for they are not intended to be academic disquisitions, but remarks, comments, prompts to reflection merely – or goads when they provoke disagreement. Their purpose is not to tell readers what to think, only to remark what has been thought (and sometimes what their author thinks) about some of the things that matter in the debate in question.

As with the contents of its predecessor volume – *The Meaning of Things* – most of the essays here began life in the *Guardian* newspaper's Saturday Review. In their weekly appearance on the back page of that Review their usual (though not invariable) intention was to apply considerations of philosophy to concrete situations in life. That remains the aim here.

I have included essays from other sources too, and a few pieces that began as book reviews, chosen because the books that stimulated them add much to the topics under discussion. And because books, and the reading and criticising of books, are a significant vehicle for the debate society has with itself, I have included discussion about reading and reviewing – not just to remind us of Lichtenberg's remark that 'a book is a mirror: if an ass peers in do not expect an apostle to look out', but because Milton is right when he says that books 'contain a potency of life in them to be as active as the souls whose progeny they are' – bearing in mind that they are the progeny as much of readers' as of authors' souls.

I have also taken the liberty of including an autobiographical reminiscence, to describe one route into a consuming interest in literary and philosophical matters – prompted by the feeling that, if one is going to write about applying philosophy to life, one might at least show how it first reached into one's own life.

In introducing this collection's predecessor I commented on Socrates' celebrated view that the best life is the considered life. He meant that an unprincipled, feckless life is so much at the mercy of chance, and so dependent on the choices made by others, that it is of little real value to the person living it. He further meant that a thoughtful life is shaped by aims and strengthened by integrity, so that, to the fullest extent possible for creatures caught in the webs of society and history, it is lived with purpose. After making these points I likened reflection to inspecting a map before a journey, which, although it is not the same thing as travelling, at least provides necessary orientation. 'A person who does not think about life is like a stranger mapless in a foreign land,' so the simile ended; 'for one such, lost and without directions, any turning in the road is as good as any other, and if it takes him somewhere worthwhile it will have done so by the merest chance.' Chance can sometimes be a happy giver, and no one should shut the door against serendipity; but Matthew Arnold implies better counsel when he says, 'They, believe me, who await/ No gifts from chance, have conquered fate.'

Moral Matters

Emotion

In the form of old wives' tales, saws, assumptions and superstitions, mankind has accumulated a vast miscellany of
wisdom and folly in its history. Folly tends to predominate over
wisdom because it is usually easier to understand and more
convenient (or exciting) to believe; but a little reflection usually
sifts one from the other.

Sometimes, however, investigation reveals genuine insights
in beliefs which at first appeared vague and only anecdotally
supported. One such is the effect of emotion on health. There
is now serious scientific scrutiny of this commonplace belief,
bringing medicine, neuroscience, microbiology and psychology
together to explore how stress and depression might make us
sick, and whether an optimistic outlook can help us either
protect against, or more effectively recover from, illness.

Although medical professionals have always recognised that
states of the body affect states of mind – a simple proof is the
way psychotropic drugs alter mood, as indeed do foodstuffs,
dancing, the weather, and everything besides – and have also
accepted the general belief that, somehow, the causal chain
works in reverse too, in the direction mind-to-body, it is only
now that proper research has begun into quantifiable questions

about how this second and more mysterious direction works – and has started looking at the most likely places, viz. the three subtle and hugely complex communication networks of hormones, the nervous system, and the immune system. Among the benefits that might result from this research is a way of combining psychological with physical therapies to enhance the latter's effectiveness, perhaps even – in the case of stubbornly depressive or pessimistic personalities – by combining psychotherapy with antibiotics, hypotensives, or whatever was required for the physical affliction in question.

The quickening of scientific interest in the emotions has included work by cognitive psychologists, whose studies on the influence of feelings on reasoning have found that just as too much emotion is bad for reasoning, so is too little. They show that the dispassionate Mr Spock of *Star Trek* would be a liability if he existed, because he lacks the kind of responses which conduce to good decisions and effective action in normal circumstances.

The role of emotion in reasoning has long been negatively viewed. Since Plato, most philosophers have held that emotions interfere with rationality. Plato likened the thinking part of the soul to a charioteer driving two powerful horses, each representing an emotional aspect of the self: one is aspirational and tries to fly up to heaven, the other is appetitive and plunges wildly towards earth. Reason, the charioteer, struggles to bring them into harmony – and to make them fly upwards together.

Stoicism was the school of philosophy which formed the outlook of educated men for five hundred years before the advent of Christianity. It premised the idea that mastery of the emotions is fundamental to a virtuous life. It taught that unless we cultivate indifference to what happens outside our control in the world, while at the same time strictly governing the thoughts, desires and feelings that arise within ourselves, we will never have peace of mind. This austerely self-denying view underwrites all later identification of calmness, coolness and dispassion with maturity and virtue. When stiff-upper-lipped Englishmen met whirling Dervishes or dancing Bantu, they thought them incontinent and therefore unable to govern themselves; and thought it a kindness as well as a convenience to colonise them.

But wiser reason recognises the true and great value of feeling. 'In a full heart there is room for everything,' said Antonio Porchia, 'while in an empty heart there is room for nothing.' Reason is a faculty of order and structure; the emotions can be the very opposite. 'We have hearts within,/ Warm, live, improvident, indecent hearts,' wrote Elizabeth Barrett Browning, thereby putting her finger on why it is essential to allow the emotions their place: for there has to be room for warmth and vividness, generosity and passion, which sometimes goes against prune-faced providence, and changes the world for the better as a result.

This is not to extol unreasonableness. Reason and feeling are equally great gifts, and equally necessary. If either is untempered by the other, the result can only be spiritual and intellectual impoverishment – yielding a life, as Socrates would say, scarcely worth living.

Moral Education

Only the educated are free.

EPICTETUS

One example of the moral perplexities being heaped upon us by the rapid advance of medical science is the case, not long ago, of a woman who found herself pregnant with twins, and decided to abort one of them on the grounds that she was not in a position to look after both. News of this case prompted media-inflamed outrage and a confused ensuing debate. For many people the affair exuded a bad moral odour, but there was no agreement why. For some, simply, it was because a healthy foetus was destroyed. For others it was the peculiar horror of the 'Sophie's Choice' involved. Some claimed that the woman acted irresponsibly, given her circumstances, in falling pregnant in the first place. Yet others were appalled by the poverty that makes a baby's life an unaffordable option in the contemporary rich West. And some were nauseated by the hypocrisy of the 'pro-lifers' who offered the pregnant woman money to keep both foetuses, in view of the links between their lobby and political views indifferent to poverty in general.

To most commentators this lack of agreement was a mark of moral disarray, of collapse in agreement about where the horizons of acceptable conduct lie. They claimed to see an emerging pattern in episodes of moral disquiet such as this one, whether caused by child murderers, gun massacres, or dilemmas about sexual abuse: namely, the aptness of a single shocking event to cause public panic, a sense that certainties have been lost and that a moral abyss is opening.

Such panic goes with belief that, until recently, there were higher and more widely shared moral standards in our society, making it a safer – indeed, a comfortable – place to be. Usually people think that this golden age of goodness and certainty came to an end with the passing of their grandparents' or parents' generations.

This belief is of course false, and it rests on a large degree of historical ignorance. Earlier times and other places indeed sometimes enjoyed spells of moral consensus, usually because of an imposed religious hegemony over thought. But consensus has never been durable; moral outlooks change with time, and human beings have always worried mightily about the fact. For example: Victorian London was a far more violent place than it is now, and it was cankered by child prostitution, drunkenness and beggary to degrees that, despite various endeavours to return us to so-called 'Victorian values', are still unimaginable.

Despite the social progress that had since been made, it remains true that society falls into moral panics, and with troubling swiftness. There are many reasons for this, among which is the now familiar one that until recently some subjects were taboo, and so did not provide the popular media with profit opportunities. The media no longer hesitate to whip up lurid anxieties in order to increase sales, in the process undermining social confidence and multiplying fears.

But a more important reason – so commentators observe – is that moral panics occur because the increased availability of information about what happens in our society is not matched by a public capacity to reflect upon and make sense of it. Western societies might be advanced in many ways, but if the standard of debate set by the popular media is anything to go by, their populations are woefully bad at engaging sensibly with new and evolving moral demands.

This last remark is not meant to imply that there are, say, too few religious education lessons in schools. Far from it: religion is part of the problem, not the solution. And moral education is not best done by haranguing people, especially the young. On both counts standard views about moral education need rethinking.

Religion is worse than an irrelevance as regards the inculcation of morality, for the following reasons: in an individualistic society, where personal wealth is the chief if not the sole measure of achievement, a morality that enjoins you to give your all to the poor, that says it is easier for a camel to go through a needle's eye than for the rich to enter heaven, and preaches selflessness towards one's neighbour and complete obedience to a deity – such a morality, wholly opposed to the norms and practices not just accepted but extolled in our society, has little to offer. Most people ignore the contrast between such views and the universal instruction to go forth and multiply one's income and possessions; and obey the latter.

And when religious fundamentalists add a preparedness to incarcerate women, mutilate genitals, amputate hands, murder, bomb, and terrorise – all in the name of faith – then religious morality becomes not just irrelevant but dangerous. With such examples and contrasts, it has less than nothing to offer proper moral debate.

Granted that admonition, whether from pulpit, lectern or hustings, is not the way to promote moral understanding, how then should it be taught? The answer is an old one: by providing and promoting liberal education, which – despite the many obstacles put in its way – has in fact had much success in making the world a better place.

Some preliminaries are required before the idea of liberal education and its ethical promise can be explained. We first need to slip the bonds of the narrow definition of 'morality' as this notion is contemporarily understood, and return to the richer and more inclusive classical conception of 'ethics'. The notion of morality applies just to part of life; for example, to the undesirability of sexual infidelity or lying. No one thinks that culinary preferences are a moral matter, nor how a person works, nor what colour clothing he wears. The ancient Greeks took a different view. For them the whole of life is an ethical matter: living well and flourishingly involves all aspects of life, and one's well-being and the effect one has on others stems from one's total character. For this reason life has to be considered – the Socratic demand again – and to be considered it has to be informed. This is where liberal education comes in.

By a liberal education is meant one that includes the arts and humanities as well as science and practical subjects. Education in literature, history, and appreciation of the arts opens the possibility for us to live more reflectively and knowledgeably, especially about the nature and variety of human experience. That, in turn, increases our capacity for understanding others better, so that we can treat them with respect and sympathy, however different their outlook on life. When sympathy and respect are returned, the result is that the differences which cause friction, even conflict, come to be resolved or at least tolerated.

This belief is doubtless utopian; and of course there have always been bad people who relished the arts; so liberal education does not automatically produce better humans. But it can be expected to do so far more often than the ignorance and egoism which arise from paucity of knowledge and lack of insight.

Liberal education is disappearing in the English-speaking West, as expectations decline and schooling narrows into training focused mainly on participation in the life of the economy. It is worth iterating what a loss this is; for the aim of liberal education is to help people continue learning all their lives long, and to think, and to question. New and challenging moral dilemmas are always likely to arise, so we need to try to make ourselves the kind of people who can respond thoughtfully. The alternative is the moral disarray that surrounded the 'aborted twin' case, and other similar panics of recent times.

Emancipation and Ethics

Art raises its head where creeds relax.

NIETZSCHE

Modern times began with a revolution – the Reformation of the sixteenth century – and have been driven along since by the many major revolutions that followed: the English seventeenth-century Cromwellian and Glorious revolutions, the scientific and Enlightenment revolutions, the American and French revolutions (in France there were several more in the century following 1789), the turmoil of 1848, Darwin, Freud, the twentieth century's exponential growth of scientific knowledge, the increasingly catastrophic European wars of the last two hundred years, the Russian revolution – the list is a long one. As the list grows, the true nature of the last five centuries emerges; we see that it has been a seething and often violent tumult. Yet the art and ideas, and the cultural personalities, of this period are the stuff of our own personal histories, for the obvious but inescapable reason that they make us and our world what they are. Anyone who sought to write an autobiography in fully express detail, therefore, would be pressed to do it justice in less than a dozen of volumes – for it would need to begin at least with the Reformation, and it would not have ended even with the twentieth century's melange of communism, nationalism, separatism, mass production, democracy, artistic experimentation, haste, holocaust, despair, and hope.

Yes, hope: for some, bravely, have found this tumultuous period a source of optimism for the future, seeing it as a history – despite everything bad in it – of burgeoning culture and increasing human emancipations of various kinds. Not even the best efforts of despots and religious fanatics have reduced this power to spread emancipation, although they are the prime cause of its unevenness of pace and reach, and its frequent back-slidings.

But emancipation is always at risk from the usual sources – demagogues, civil and international war, the tenure that superstitions have over the human imagination – so there are no guarantees that progress will continue. If it does continue, one main reason will be increasing commerce between people, and the wealth and understanding it brings. Another will be the yeasting power of education, when it takes people beyond the rudiments required for playing a part in the contemporary economy, and opens to them the possibilities of culture. Significantly, the revolutions which have impelled history in the last five hundred years have all either been, or have fundamentally influenced, the culture of that part of the world which, in this period, was the chief engine of change: Europe.

I use the term 'culture' in a non-anthropological sense to mean the human practices and products which civilise – that is, which add amenity, insight, pleasure, significance and value to individual and social existence through excellences of thought, performance, and artefact. Culture in this sense is connected to ethics, not as either a necessary or a sufficient condition for any individual's doing good to others, but as a necessary condition for the possibility of there being good lives to be lived by individuals.

What is the relation of culture – and especially the arts – and most especially the narrative arts – and most especially among them novels and the drama – to the moral life? The obvious answer, though no less true for being so, is that acquaintance with literature and the arts enlarges one's insight into the human condition, and thus serves as a powerful adjunct to promoting the sympathies which are part of the necessary basis for morality.

The argument is as follows. Jack will act in ways which recognise, and are sensitive to, Jill's interests, only if he is able to grasp how things are for Jill, and understands why they matter to her; and, further, recognises that things being that way for Jill makes a claim on some of his own attitudes and behaviour.

Any Jack's gaining access to any Jill's perspective on life thus demands a degree of sympathy. But when Jill's interests and aims lie outside the normal range of Jack's own experience, his ability to sympathise with Jill's concerns enough to be considerate about them in relevant ways, will require him to see beyond his own usual range. Most people can learn about the needs and interests of others by extrapolating from their own experience and from their observation of people around them; but if these were the only resources for insight, the scope of an individual's sympathies would be limited. And this is where the narrative arts come in. Exposure to the narrative arts overcomes that limitation: it enormously widens an attentive individual's perceptions of human experience, and enables him – vicariously, or as a fly-on-the-wall witness – to see into lives, conditions and experiences which he might never encounter in practice. This extension and education of the sympathies is therefore the basis for a richer moral experience and a more refined capacity for moral response.

An immediate problem with these thoughts is that there were no doubt SS officers at Auschwitz who returned from their day's work to read Goethe and listen to Beethoven on the gramophone. Does this not destroy the link between art and the good life? Might it not be that Plato is right, and that art in fact destroys or at least threatens to undermine morality? Well: the example certainly shows that appreciation of art is not *sufficient* for an individual's doing good to others. But that was not in any case the claim. The claim is that educating moral sensibility through imagination has a general tendency, not a universal effect, and works by heightening morally relevant insight in at least many cases, in not all of which will the insight necessarily conduce to the good (after all, the sadist has to have insight into his victim's circumstances in order to do what he does; so mere possession of the insight is also not a guarantee of such goods as kindness and consideration). But it is more likely to do so than to leave questions of how to get along with others to the tender education of ignorance, greed, unbridled competition and strife.

The education of moral sensibility with regard to the question of how we should treat others is only part of the story. The other part of the story is the quality of an individual's own life as he experiences it. Here too the narrative arts have an enormous amount to offer. The idea of making one's life worthwhile by choosing goals and striving towards them, sometimes deferring present satisfactions in the hope of greater rewards later, demands the imposition of a narrative structure upon it, as if one were the author of one's own story. And only by being aware of a rich array of possible narratives and goals to choose from can one's choices and actions be truly informed and maximally free. Once again, exposure to stories – which in part represent possible lives – is a vital ingredient in the ethical construction of an individual's personal future history.

It might be argued that part of what makes a work of fiction, painting or theatre a work of *art* is precisely its potential to be a significant element in the interaction between narratives and lives which make certain narratives (or narrative types) immensely important to us, and life-enriching in ways closely related to the two just canvassed. But that raises a question, 'What is art?', which belongs to another debate.

Symbols

A person gets from a symbol the meaning he puts into it, and what is one man's comfort and inspiration is another's jest and scorn

JUSTICE JACKSON

Robert Mapplethorpe's famous photograph of a lily is disturbing and erotic precisely because lilies, as symbols of purity, are more often seen in tender religious iconography than in homosexual art representing male organs efflorescing in pleasure. The power and ambiguity of symbols is well illustrated by an extraordinary controversy over another use to which lilies were put, this time as a symbol of Catholic nationalism in Northern Ireland. To the fury of Protestant Loyalists, lilies were planted in the grounds of Stormont Castle, the home of the Northern Ireland Assembly; and their presence was accordingly interpreted by Ulstermen as an insult.

Northern Ireland is a land of symbols, each made potent and terrible by history. Loyalist symbols include the colour orange, the bowler hat, poppies, the crown, and the fearsome Red Fist. The date 1690 and the slogan 'No Surrender' are also frequent symbols in the mural paintings marking Loyalist territory. They recall the victory of William of Orange, securer of the Protestant succession to the British crown, over his Catholic rivals at the Battle of the Boyne in 1690. For Ulstermen – descendants of Scottish Protestant settlers in the northern part of Ireland from the early seventeenth century onward – they are essential marks of identity and survival.

Nationalist symbols include the colour green, the O'Neill coat of arms, the harp, the date 1916 – and the Easter Lily, the two latter recalling the uprising in that same year. They connect Nationalists to the long history of colonisation by the English – and sometimes of brutal oppression by them, as at the hands of Cromwell.

The sanctity acquired by symbols, and the fierce emotions they rouse, are familiar from religious controversies. In China's Cultural Revolution temples were destroyed and much devotional art lost through the zeal of Communist atheism, but a far worse iconoclasm destroyed almost all the religious art in England during the Puritan epoch, as an expression of anti-Catholicism. Yet everywhere in Christendom the cross remained a potent, indeed a magic, symbol, the mere gesturing of which was taken to bless, heal, protect and sanctify.

A symbol is a token which carries meaning, often an entire world of meaning, not necessarily because it resembles or portrays the thing symbolised, but because of the associations it raises in the mind of anyone who grasps its conventional significance. The word 'symbol' has its roots in a Greek term denoting a half-token which, when reunited with its other half, established the identity of its possessor. By generalisation the term has come to apply to anything which, in a simple and (so to speak) portable way, systematically stands for something very much more complex than itself. Road-signs illustrate the point well: if a driver sees a simplified picture of a petrol-pump, he knows that fuel and other motoring amenities lie close ahead.

The power of symbols to convey much by minimal means has been central to the growth of knowledge. Arguably, the truly distinctive feature of human intelligence is its ability to create and use them. A classic case concerns mathematical symbols. It is one thing to recognise the difference between three apples and five pears, but quite another to grasp all the relationships that exist between 3 and 5: that the latter is 2 more than the former, that one multiplied by the other yields 15, while summed they produce 8 – and so on. The abstract properties of collections of things would be impossible to investigate without the simple but immensely powerful symbolic notation of arithmetic. The Romans did not have a symbol for nothing (zero), and were so hampered by the lack that they were incapable of contributing to mathematical knowledge.

In an extended sense, the role of words in language, and concepts in the realm of thought, is to stand for things, events, complexes and operations other than themselves. The philosopher John Locke was the first to see clearly that almost all knowledge is concerned with general ideas and the relations between them, and that language is the system in which ideas are expressed and employed. Not all words are symbols (many are purely functional devices, like 'and' and 'the'), but those that denote objects and events in the world operate in the same way as symbols, and like their arithmetical counterparts make it possible to bring what is distant in time and space directly before the mind, liberating thought from the confines of immediate experience. In this freedom lies the source of the human intellectual adventure.

For most, mention of symbols suggests signs or objects (like the Christian cross or Islamic crescent) which have a particular cultural and sometimes emotional significance, prompting responses shared by most other people in the same cultural tradition. To enjoy a visit to a Western art gallery fully, one has to understand at least the rudiments of the symbolism that abounds in the art treasures it contains. A picture of a woman in a blue robe, with a child on her knee who raises two fingers to a man dressed in animal skins and a woman holding a wheel, is immediately identifiable as a picture of the Virgin and infant Christ, the latter blessing St John the Baptist (who lived a feral life, eating locusts and honey) and St Catherine (who was martyred by being broken on a wheel). Ignorance of the symbols – blue for the Virgin, the wheel for Catherine – renders the picture's meaning opaque.

Symbols have the unfortunate power to acquire the importance of what they symbolise. They become objects of veneration or hatred in their own right, and it becomes a sin (or, for enemies, a virtue) to mistreat them. Some people express anti-American feeling, for example, by burning the Stars and Stripes, an action contrasting sharply with the respectful handling of the flag in US military ceremonies. The very concept of 'desecration' – of mishandling or disrespectfully treating a symbolically important object or place – depends crucially on the power of symbols to share the reality of what they symbolise.

Worst of all, symbols sometimes live on in their own right when what they symbolise has long been forgotten. It is an intriguing and dismaying parlour game to itemise the symbols that have become their own reality, and to count how many there are; for people not only live by symbols, but die by them, as wars of religion and nationalism attest.

As this suggests, the one symbol whose meaning is too often forgotten or ignored, yet most needs to stand at every crossroads, is the white dove, icon of peace.

Religion

There is only one religion, though there are a hundred versions of it.

SHAW

Four kinds of answer are standardly given to the question why religion exists. One is that it provides explanations – of the origin of the universe, of the way it works, of the apparently inexplicable things that happen in it, and of why it includes evil and suffering. Another is that religion provides comfort, giving hope of life after death, providing reassurance in a hostile world, and a means (by supplication, propitiation, and the practice of one or another form of prescribed behaviour) to get a better deal in it. A third is that it makes for social order, in promoting morality and social cohesion. And a fourth is that it rests on the natural ignorance, stupidity, superstitiousness and gullibility of mankind.

Among those who strongly disagree that these are the right explanations are, of course, religious folk, who think that there is religion because there is a god – or gods; and perhaps spirits and ancestors too – and that therefore religious belief is the natural and obvious response to this alleged fact. But there are others who, without being in the slightest religious, also do not think that the standard answers are right.

One such is Pascal Boyer, an anthropologist who has studied the Fang people of Cameroon. But he is an anthropologist with a difference, for he has also studied and assimilated the research done in recent decades in neurophysiology, psychology and cognitive science, which has jointly given us a greatly improved understanding of the way mental life functions, in important part by enhancing our understanding of the brain. As these remarks suggest, Boyer's principal claim is that religion is the result of the way the brain works. Brains are very complicated mechanisms for processing information and drawing inferences. These tasks are carried out by a large number of specialist subsystems which operate at deep levels of the brain's structure. In fact, the greatest part of the work done by the brain occurs in this way, out of sight of the conscious mind. Using a small number of 'ontological categories' which classify things in the world into five orders – animals, plants, tools, natural objects and persons – the subroutines of the brain form expectations, make guesses and draw inferences, thus allowing the brain to represent the world to itself, and to interpret it.

The psychological organisation of the mind does not need anything special or additional to create religious concepts, Boyer argues; all the materials for doing so already exist in the way it works. Because minds can detach concepts from their normal settings and yet retain most of the standard inferential connections that accompany them, they can easily generate notions of the supernatural. For example: a spirit is a being which cannot be seen, and can pass through walls – and thus is different from ordinary animals and persons – but it can hear and see what we do, and interact with us in other ways – thus retaining the normal characteristics of animals and persons.

Using this explanatory paradigm, Boyer asks why religious beliefs are about gods and spirits, why such beliefs matter, why death figures so largely in them, why they involve rituals, and why they give rise to fundamentalism and violence. A persistent corollary of Boyer's answers to all these questions is that religion is a practical matter for most people, who in most cultures do not regard it as something odd or different from their other beliefs about the world. And, he says, most people are in fact vague about what they believe, and do not have a polished theology to account for their commitments and practices.

All this is undoubtedly true, and there is no better account of the way mental phenomena arise than the computational theory Boyer describes. It is a theory extremely well supported by empirical research. As an explanation of how concepts are formed, including religious ones, it is especially illuminating and powerful. But it does not provide an explanation of religion. For the standard explanations described above are consistent with the account Boyer gives, and are not displaced by it.

The reasons are many, but one merits special mention. Culture is not merely an epiphenomenal outcome of computational systems in human brains, but in part at least is the result of feedback upon those systems by the high-level concepts and practices which earlier mental activity produced. Culture assumes an existence of its own outside the individuals who make it or subscribe to it, and it affects them as much as they affect it. The majority of people may be passive consumers or spectators of culture, but significant minorities have a crucial influence on cultural development and content – chiefly: religious leaders, demagogues, writers, and thinkers – and the ordinarily vague grasp of the majority is a set of diluted versions of what these few have wrought. Boyer offers a mechanism for the formulation of the types of concepts that figure in religious culture, but the 'how' of their formation does not explain why they, rather than close competitors, acquire the special grip they do in concrete historical and social circumstances. Why, for example, have traditionally conceived deities had human characteristics of will, intention, memory and emotion, instead of being like (say) waterfalls, carrots or birds? The reasons are assuredly cultural and conscious, and not in themselves a function of underlying brain activity – which is indifferently able to do the cross-connecting which would allow a carrot to pass through a wall and still taste like a carrot, as it allows the gods to see through a wall yet be able to observe a person sinning behind it.

Much of Boyer's argument is premised on the reflex, unthe-oretical character of religious belief displayed in the sort of societies anthropologists typically study – the Fang of Cameroon and the Kwaio of the Solomon Islands, for example – but it might be seriously misleading to think that such peoples get us closer to unadulterated evidence than do, say, Western Christians and Jews. These latter have highly articulated religious literatures and traditions, which provide a rich vein of material other than the subroutines of the brain for thinking about why religions exist – not least in explicitly offering themselves as elaborate theories about origins, morality, and the rest, exactly as the standard accounts of religion say.

Credity

Each believes easily what he fears and what he desires.
LA FONTAINE

Credulity, insecurity and desire form a potent combination in the human psyche. Together they make us eager to believe any nonsense if it purports to yield a glimpse of the future, or offers even the slenderest hope of success in love or fortune. On this rests the livelihood of many tricksters and charlatans – the crystal-ball gazers, palmists, astrologers, and readers of tarot cards.

Tarot is not, properly speaking, a divinatory practice, but a complex card game, invented in the fifteenth century, which, somewhat like bridge, turns on capturing tricks. Originally called 'trionfi' ('triumphs' or 'trumps') it involves – as the name suggests, and again like bridge – trump cards which capture tricks by outvaluing other cards played to the table. The standard tarot pack consists of 78 cards, of which 56 are distributed into four sequentially numbered suits called Cups, Coins, Swords and Batons, each of which has four Court cards (a Knight joins the usual three). The remaining 22 are non-suited picture cards, and they constitute what is distinctive about the tarot pack. One, the Fool, stands by itself; the other 21 are numbered in sequence and depict such subjects as a Hanged Man, a Devil, a Wheel of Fortune, the Moon, a Pope, and an Emperor.

In 1980 the philosopher Michael Dummett published a book on the game of tarot, taking pains to distance it from the occult and divinatory uses to which tarot cards have been put. Recognising later that his strictures had gone unheeded, he returned to the fray, aided by two collaborators, and published another book to show definitively and finally that occult applications of tarot cards are not only bunkum but exceedingly recent bunkum, dating from the late eighteenth and nineteenth centuries. So successful is their onslaught that Dummett and his fellow-authors not only demolish the occult tarot but (so to speak) the whole house of cards involving magic, alchemy, Rosicrucianism, fortune-telling, and the rest of the so-called 'Higher Sciences' invented by febrile intelligence. They do so by implication, almost as an aside; for merely to know how these imaginative theories arose, and how they came to be applied in the occult use of tarot cards, is to see them for what they are.

If a single individual is responsible for the current popularity of the occult tarot it is the nineteenth-century charlatan Eliphas Levi, who synthesised the ideas of eighteenth-century predecessors into an elaborate theory. Those predecessors – such men as Court de Gébelin and 'Etteila' (a Parisian entrepreneur called Aliette who first coined the term 'cartonomancie') – exploited the heady mixture of Hermeticism, Rosicrucianism, alchemy and the Cabala first brewed in the Renaissance, and added a mystical form of more recent interest in Egyptology. Among the resulting beliefs were that tarot cards constitute a secret book of the universe, from a reading of which *everything* can be learned. We think of eighteenth-century France as the crucible of Enlightenment; yet it was simultaneously awash with Freemasonry and interest in the occult, especially in the latter half of the century. There is no contradiction here; every movement of thought carries its opposites with it.

Levi developed a theory out of this rapidly evolving 'tradition', formulating a Cabalistic tarot in opposition to Etteila's Hermetic one. But it was left to a disciple – one Gerard Encausse, who called himself 'Papus' – to popularise it, for whereas Levi had few literary skills, Papus could write. He systematised Levi's teachings, and his writings inaugurated the practice of occult tarot known today.

The key to the tarot pack's divinatory use is the enigmatic and somewhat chilling array of figures on the trumps. 'The Hanged Man', 'The Wheel of Fortune', 'The Devil' hint darkly at mysteries, and they prompt a frisson. In his earlier book Dummett commented that whatever they meant to their first devisers, the private meanings of these figures are now lost. But this of course is exactly why they are now so apt for occult purposes. They beautifully illustrate the recipe for nonsense, which is: take something strange-looking, whose meaning is now forgotten, and liberally stir in imagination and superstition. In this respect the divinatory tarot is a paradigm of all superstitions and wonderfully illustrates humanity's clever, ingenious, and intricate capacity for folly.

Fasting

Holy periods are well observed: the rich keep the feasts and the poor keep the fasts.

SYDNEY SMITH

Fasting at certain times of year is a practice very ancient and widespread in human cultures. It has become annexed to religious observance, the Lent of Christianity and the Ramadan of Islam noticeable among them. Some Christian churches distinguish carefully between fasting and abstinence, Catholics defining the former as restriction to one meal a day (with two supplementary meals, if necessary, but not jointly amounting to a second full meal), the latter as eating no meat. In this sense Buddhism is always abstinent, and its serious monks fast perpetually.

Where fasting means not eating during daylight hours, as in Ramadan, calculating when dawn and sunset occur becomes a fine matter. Whereas many religions emphasise the importance of fasting as a spiritual exercise – hypoglycaemia can cause other-worldly sensations, being a form of endogenous intoxication, and consisting mainly of light-headedness – they also recognise its health benefits. And it is in these that fasting as a deliberate practice, rather than an economic accident, probably began.

In Europe the season of plenty was, historically, winter. A sentimental picture suggests itself: with the harvest in, the pigs fattened, the stores replete with salted meat and straw-packed apples, it was the time when, with little to be done out of doors, people sat together round the fire, making clothes and mending tools while they exchanged stories and songs. With the onset of spring – 'Lent' comes from 'lengthening', denoting the increasing hours of daylight – the stores had begun to deplete, requiring economies, and anyway people were stiff and heavy from lack of exercise, which they especially felt as they cleaned their stuffy houses. So the spring was a period of purgation, and the emptying stores heralded the onset of the hungriest part of the year – summer – the time before the harvest, while the cattle were still suckling their young.

Nature, not the supernatural, thus first ordained Lent, and no doubt the empirical and observant eye of some intelligent individual noted that those who had to tighten their belts periodically tended to be healthier than those whose stores – and therefore bellies – were always full. This was certainly so among the folk of classical antiquity, whose physicians prescribed fasting and purgation as the surest remedies once illness had come, and moderation and abstinence as a way of preventing it altogether.

Interestingly, the light and healthful Mediterranean diet has not given rise to anything like the cultural phenomenon typical of countries where heavy dumplings, meat and beer are a staple – namely, the Spa resort, where a year's residuum of those sluggish viands are scoured from the bowels of Central Europeans by hot mineral waters. The Spas became a wonderful institution in the centuries before modern medicine, not just because their waters and treatments helped combat the costive diet and Biedermeyer excess of their patrons, but because they were centres of culture. Carlsbad, strung like pearls along the winding banks of the Tepla in a fold of Bohemia's wooded hills, boasts the oldest orchestra in Europe. Beethoven and Goethe were regular visitors there, to sip the ambiguously tasting product of the springs and to bathe in them. At one end of the valley stands a magnificent hostelry, the Grandhotel Pupp, a palace of a bygone age of splendour and repose. As an alternative to Lent, forty days at the Pupp is much preferable, the purgations it offers anything but purgatorial.

It is hard to imagine how the Russian novel could have got along without German spas, since so many of them seem to have been written in places like Baden Baden and Marienbad. Turgenev wandered from one to another, thinking about fathers, sons and first love, and Dostoevsky struggled to purge his gambling addiction in them.

One virtue of fasting in the Islamic view is that it teaches us how the poor and hungry feel. That is a good discipline. Perhaps 'the cleannesse of sweet abstinence', as George Herbert put it, is as medicinal to the moral sense as it is to the body. If so, it is the real reason why it might make people better.

Meat

*It is useless for the sheep to pass resolutions in favour of
vegetarianism while the wolf is of a different opinion.*

INGE

There is something ancient and dreadful about the pyres of
burning animals which reddened the English nights during
the country's great self-induced crisis, at the beginning of the
twenty-first century, over 'foot and mouth' disease in its herds
of cattle. The pyres were reminiscent of classical antiquity's
largest exercise in holy sacrifice, the hecatomb, in which a
hundred oxen were slaughtered and burned to elicit the gods'
favour. In those days that number of beasts represented an
immense oblation of self-impoverishment by the community,
undertaken to prove its earnest to the gods. (Such things still
happen; the Taliban of Afghanistan sacrificed cows to apologise
to God for taking so long to destroy some ancient and beautiful
Buddhist statues in their care – thus annoying not only Bud-
dhists but also Hindus, for whom cows are sacred.)

Our more recent burnt offerings addressed a single god,
Mammon, who does not care that the slaughtered beasts had
little wrong with them physically, but who hates the vileness
of their economic disease: reduced yields of milk and meat
leading to reduced profits.

Some newspapers spoke of angry farmers guarding their cherished herds against the cull. Cynics claimed that the impression

given was misleading. Every normal week more than half a million animals die in abattoirs in England, so it was not the vast industry of death which the farmers contested, said the cynics, but the fact that they got less money for vet-slaughtered than abattoir-butchered beasts.

From Cumbrian foot-and-mouth pyres to the thousands of acres of grazing that were once Amazonian forest, from cardiology wards tending fat-clogged heart to lorries crammed with bleating lambs on their way to slaughter, the costs of meat-eating are immense. The arguments against it are severally persuasive and jointly compelling. There is an economic argument, which points out that two people can be fed from an acre of land on which livestock are run, as against twenty if it is cultivated for grain. There is a health argument, which points out that meat is full of fat and bacteria, and if non-organic then full also of growth hormones, antibiotics and vaccines. And strongest of all there is a moral argument, against killing sentient creatures for our pleasure, when we do not need to do so to live wisely and well.

It is prudent to take the health argument seriously. We do not eat 'fresh' meat, we eat carrion, for the former would be stiff with rigor mortis, and meat only becomes soft enough to cook and eat once it has begun to rot. We like our game especially rotten, which is why we leave it hanging for days so that the microbes swarming in it can do their work. Microbes are the meat-eater's friend; without them there could be no tender steak, no juicy roast, no tasty chop or rib. To see how they work, put a dead mouse in the garden and watch what happens. The little corpse decomposes with such fury that it seems to be wriggling and trying to run away, such is the pullulating mass of microbes consuming it within. Once the proteins in a corpse have become cheesy, the 'cheese skippers' (*piophila casei*) arrive to do what they do to old cheese (and dirty feet – which is why the French call choice gorgonzola *les pieds de Dieu*). Everything is finished off by bacteria, which in ten hours multiply from 100 to 100 million. They are present in these numbers on the meat in your kitchen; they eat your meat as they ate the mouse, and since everything that eats must defecate, it is their lack of toilet training that gives exposed meat its gamey aroma.

The health argument is a prudential one; the moral argument is one of principle. A frank look at what is involved in rearing, transporting and killing the animals we eat daily should fill any normal person with more revulsion than the microbial tale just told. How many meat-eaters would cut the throat of a cow themselves, and hack open its belly with a knife to empty its intestines? But the thousands of daily deaths of animals are hidden away, and on the butcher's shelf meat looks innocuous, nothing like the living thing it was. It is odd: we prosecute anyone who is cruel to a cow – by beating it or giving it electric shocks, say – yet the connection between that fact and the dinner table is rarely made.

Evil

He who accepts evil without protesting against it is really co-operating with it.

MARTIN LUTHER KING

'Evil' is first and foremost a religious notion. It means whatever a religion dislikes. Christianity assimilated various pagan deities and practices when obliged to make concessions to stubborn peasant predilections (hence the incorporation of Diana worship into Catholic veneration of the Virgin Mary), but it otherwise proscribed all other and earlier deities as devils. The chief devil, Satan, is himself a composite figure. He is Lucifer, he is the Green man of pagan nature beliefs, he is the lusty goat-footed satyr who sported with nymphs in the groves of antiquity. He is, in short, the representative and personification of things the church wished people to stop liking and doing.

As Lucifer, the devil began as a grand and beautiful angel whose sin was disobedience – a frightful crime in religious eyes: for the height of virtue is unquestioning obedience to God's will, whatever it is (even if God tells you to cut your child's throat, as in the Abraham story). Milton liked Lucifer's desire for autonomy and self-expression, and for his resulting rebellion against the absolutist oppression of God; which is why the poetry of *Paradise Lost* soars, as if on archangels' wings, whenever Lucifer – Milton's tragic hero – is central to the action.

As the Green Man, satyr, or any supernatural figure not sanctioned by orthodoxy as angel or saint, Satan represents forces of nature and aspects of the world which the church wishes to suppress, chief among them the appetites for sex and pleasure. To do this it employs the time-honoured trick of demonising them and making people afraid of them, portraying them as ugly and dangerous. (Governments do the same in propaganda about enemies in times of war.) And then, to sink the roots of this fear deep, the church introduces the idea of evil and the devil to children, for it knows that if it can cut early psychological scars it has a better chance of holding on to the minds thus wounded.

All religions are anxious to proselytise the young. Society seems not to see either the absurdity or the danger in the fact that pupils in one school are taught, as truths of history, that the Normans conquered England in 1066 and that Jesus is the son of God, in another that the Normans conquered England in 1066 and Jesus is not the son of God but that Mohammed received the definitive divine revelation, in a third that the Normans conquered England in 1066 and that neither Jesus nor Mohammed is of any significance besides Guru Dev – and in a fourth that the Normans conquered England in 1066 and all three of Jesus, Mohammed and Guru Dev are false distractions, attention to whom is likely to provoke God's jealous wrath.

Yet in schools all over the country these antipathetic 'truths' are being force-fed to different groups of pupils, none of whom is in a position to assess their credibility or worth. This is a serious form of child abuse. It sows the seeds of apartheids capable of resulting, in their logical conclusion, in murder and war, as history sickeningly and ceaselessly proves.

There is no greater social evil than religion. It is the cancer in the body of humanity. Human credulity and superstition, and the need for comforting fables, will never be extirpated, so religion will always exist, at least among the uneducated. The only way to manage the dangers it presents is to confine it entirely to the private sphere, and for the public domain to be blind to it in all but one respect: that by law no one's private beliefs should be allowed to cause a nuisance or an injury to anyone else. For whenever and wherever religion manifests itself in the public arena as an organised phenomenon, it is the most Satanic of all things.

Luxury

Luxury either comes of wealth, or makes it necessary.
ROUSSEAU

Prince Jefri Bolkiah of Brunei had to auction his possessions after the collapse of his business empire in 1998, leaving him with debts of three billion dollars. It is unclear why a member of one of the world's richest families chose to engage in business in the first place (to describe the Brunei royal family as rich is like describing Everest as a pebble), but he did it anyway, perhaps for fun. When bankruptcy followed he quarrelled with his family, who would not rescue him. In the end he had to accept the sale of his possessions, and an allowance from the Sultan of Brunei of a mere 300,000 dollars a month.

Hundreds flocked from all over the world to the Prince's auction, to buy a piece of royalty and to slake their fascination with the idea of the mammoth luxury involved. On sale were gold-plated toilet-brush holders, gigantic marble jacuzzis, several grand pianos, dozens of huge television sets, and thousands of items of jewellery. An unkind observer might say that what the purchasers and their prince thought of as luxurious was what others would describe as ostentatious and excessive – invariably the way, so such an observer might say, with those who have more money than taste.

Citizens of ancient Sybaris on the Gulf of Tarentum became

a byword for luxury, so wealthy and easeful was their life. They demanded their dinner invitations a year in advance so that they could properly choose what to wear. As imperial Rome waxed fat on its conquests it followed the Sybarites' example, wealthy citizens holding stupendous banquets at which guests periodically quitted their couches to visit the vomitarium, there to make room for yet more food and wine. Seneca criticised not just the excess of his contemporaries but the effect on their sensibilities. In the third book of his *Questions about Nature* he describes the way Roman epicures liked to watch surmullets die on the dinner table before them, so that they could enjoy the beautiful changes of colour displayed as the fish suffocated.

The idea of luxury as excess – and later, under Christianity, sin – was marked in the distinction drawn by Roman thinkers between *luxus*, meaning abundance and pleasure, and *luxuria*, meaning grossness. It is the latter that weakens minds as it does bodies, pulping and pursing the tissues of thought as it softens and bloats flesh. It results from a failure to see that refinements of sensuality are not the same as ostentation and excess, and are indeed negated by them.

By sensuality is accurately meant the physical pleasure taken in colours and textures, tastes and sounds – things that delight the senses, charm and heighten them, offer them the best of what they are apt for. The eye enjoys light, tonalities, hues, shapes; the sense of touch loves silk, skin, warmth and coolness, the roughness of sand and the gliding face of marble; the ear loves harmonies and concords, melodies and rhythms, and the calmer sounds of nature such as falling water, air stirring among leaves, birdsong.

When the pleasures of the other senses are added to gustation, the result is as Isherwood describes in recognising that the little dishes and delicate instruments of a Chinese banquet are like artists' materials, as if the assembled company were going to paint rather than eat. Among the dishes are foods present for texture more than taste, such as water-chestnuts and bamboo. At informal dinners the Chinese are not so restrained; they relish instead the sight and aroma of rising steam, glistening edibles, abundance – as *luxus*, not *luxuria*.

But the senses are only conduits, and their work would have little lasting value if it did not serve something of greater significance – as materials of mind. The senses' pleasure in colour and melody is the mind's pleasure in pictures and music, and they in turn most often (though not invariably, because the mind enjoys abstraction too) prompt thought. And thought is the greatest luxury of all. It fills immensity, as Blake said; and as Emerson said, it sets you free.

Games

Our games reveal our characters.

OVID

Every weekend of the year millions of people invite the pleasure or disappointment of watching games or engaging in them, in some cases – as with the fortunes of a local football team and its stars – experiencing them as soap-opera. The interest is intense; the emotional catharses produced by incident, achievement, displays of skill, victory – even defeat – are equally so.

There is supposed to be something innocent about games. They are meant for recreation and pleasure. The very concept is defined by contrast with what is real, serious and consequential. But of course games are not invariably innocent, nor are they invariably the opposite of what is serious and consequential. The professionalisation of sport has removed the innocence from game playing in its major leagues, though the fun remains for spectators, except perhaps those who make a tenuous living by gambling on them. And in their origin games are innocent only in being make-believe, for they have the serious intent of providing practice for real life; obviously enough, lion cubs pouncing on one another are preparing themselves to rend the antelope. 'Most sorts of diversion in men, children, and other animals,' said Swift, 'are an imitation of fighting' – and therefore a preparation for the various struggles constitutive of life.

There are significant differences of meaning among the terms 'sport', 'game', 'recreation', 'diversion', 'exercise' and 'pastime'. Snakes and ladders is not a sport but a game, shooting tigers is not a game but a sport, hill walking is neither a game nor a sport, a particular instance of the sport cricket is called a game of cricket (and so for many but not all other sports) – and what is a diversion for spectators is a recreation for participants – although for professionals it is not guaranteed to be either, nor even fun; especially if they play badly or lose.

If we describe a person as 'game' we mean he is willing, courageous, adventurous. If we describe an animal as game, we mean it is the kind we hunt not just for food but for the pleasure of killing it and perhaps making a trophy of its hide or horns. Here Ovid's remark about how our diversions reflect our characters is relevant. Fox hunters say that their pleasure is well described by Trollope: the pell-mell gallop, the exhilarating hedgerow leaps, the country air fresh in their faces. They do not mention the pleasure given by the sight of one exhausted and terrified animal being bloodily savaged by many dogs. If this is part of the pleasure, they should be ashamed. If it is truly the former, then a drag hunt would do.

Wittgenstein used the analogy of games to describe the various uses of language. We use language to inform, ask, command, entertain, speculate, curse, joke, agree, reminisce, play, emote, and much besides. There is no single feature shared by all these practices, Wittgenstein claimed; just as games lack a single mutually defining feature, likewise language, in its great variety, has no essence. He therefore called uses of language 'language games'. For the analogy to work, it has to be true that there is no characteristic which any candidate activity must possess to be classifiable as a game. The point of his argument is that if language has no essence one cannot give a systematic theory to explain how it works. He was trying to bring philosophical speculation about meaning to an end.

Is Wittgenstein right about games? It is a good game trying to prove him wrong, and needs no equipment except a brain. And like many other games it has a serious and useful point.

Marriage

I fear nothing for a match of equals.

AESCHYLUS

Marriage is a public obsession hardly ever out of the news. The weddings of celebrities, and their divorces, are tabloid staples. Politicians and bishops urge it, supported by wider conservative and religious lobbies. The more that marriage seems to be in trouble as an institution, with smaller percentages entering and larger percentages leaving, the more intense becomes the *brouhaha* surrounding it.

It is regarded as a misfortune for an individual, especially for a woman, not to marry. Yet it is regarded as equally bad, if not worse, for an individual to indulge in too much marriage, whether in the form of repeated divorces and weddings, or bigamy. Failure to marry is punished in personal terms; excessive marriage is publicly punished in social, financial and even legal ways. This shows how entrenched is the traditional marital ideal of finding and faithfully adhering for life to one equally faithful member of the opposite sex.

These facts are illustrated by contemporary events. One is the conviction for bigamy of a Mormon in Utah, sentenced to years in prison because he has five wives and twenty-five children. Another is the difficulty experienced by a recent Irish Prime Minister who lived with a woman other than his wife.

When he gave an obligatory reception for a newly appointed Irish Cardinal, it proved a ticklish occasion. His partner's name appeared on the invitation, so the Cardinal responded with an admonitory speech, saying that marriage is the 'deep centre of human intimacy' and that 'the whole future of society depends' on it. These overstatements come, note, from a professional bachelor officially ignorant about marital intimacy, who by his own definition therefore contributes nothing to society's future.

In the US's Bible Belt divorce and cohabitation rates rocketed by as much as 200 per cent in the last decade of the twentieth century. One sad tale explains: 'In church they made me think the important thing was to get married and have children, then Christ would come,' said one escapee. 'I said yes to the first man who asked.'

The debate about marriage rests on a fundamental confusion. The word 'marriage' has two quite different senses. One is the socio-legal institution which in effect amounts to a tripartite contract between a man, a woman, and the state. The other is the long-term committed relationship entered into voluntarily by people who, because of their affection for one another, wish to pool resources and share the joys and burdens of life. In this latter (relationship) sense, the number and sexes of the mutual parties is no part of the definition, which turns solely on concepts of affection, choice and sharing. In the former (socio-legal) sense, considerations of the number and sexes of the parties are crucial, because it permits only one rigidly narrow view of what is acceptable, based on ancient religious views which do not reflect much about human reality or need.

Most people who wish to marry in the second (relationship) sense assume they must do so by marrying in the first (socio-legal) sense. To this mistake they add ignorance of history. The roots of socio-legal marriage lie in a profoundly sexist financial arrangement. Its originating aim was to constrain women's sexuality and fertility so that men could be sure they were bequeathing their property to their own offspring. In medieval Christianity a marriage of convenience existed between religious views about sex and social views about wealth. When poorer classes also began to acquire property, the requirements for premarital female chastity, and legal forms of marriage to make descent and property traceable, were extended to them too – notably in eighteenth-century England, whose highly various marriage traditions were at last reduced by law to a single type.

These tendentious formalities are latecomers to the scene, but human intimacy is as ancient as life itself. Marriage as a mutuality of true minds and tender hearts, so long as it lasts, is the happiest of states, whatever the number and gender of the parties to it; and the only effect that marriage in the socio-legal sense has had on marriage in this deeper sense, is usually to spoil it.

Sex

Love's mysteries in souls do grow; but yet the body is his book.
JOHN DONNE

A common thread connects opposition to contraception, erotically flavoured advertising, hostility to minority sexual lifestyles, and complaints about sex in film and art – and such opposition still goes on, even in the supposedly enlightened modern world. The common thread is 'Mrs Grundyism', the moral conservatism which presumes to tell other people what to think and how to behave.

Perhaps such conservatism should now take its name from the late Mary Whitehouse or some other more recent champion in the great cause of making people as sexually inactive, ignorant, and powerless as possible. What such warriors wish is to stop people having sex unless thoroughly married, to stop people knowing anything about it if unmarried (and not much more if they are), and – anyway for orthodox Catholics – to put people completely at the mercy of reproductive chance despite the availability of safe scientific means of controlling fertility. This is what the anti-sex crusade desires: limitation, ignorance, enslavement to biology, and marginalisation of sex to hidden places in just one conventional kind of relationship.

If sexual relations are ever perfunctory and unimaginative, unsatisfying or downright frustrating, exploitative, furtive, sleazy or violent, it will have a great deal to do with the meddling hand of moralism. If there is a troubling level of sexually trans-mitted disease in society, it will again have much to do with moralism. If there are unwanted pregnancies, especially among single girls and young women, and a high rate of abortions, it will yet again be because of moralism. Why? Because of the counterproductive effect of moralism's futile endeavour to limit and control sexuality by denial, by limiting knowledge and opportunity, and by directing the sexual side of human nature into as anodyne and routine a channel as possible. Moralists think that if they expose people – and especially the young, those volcanoes of hormones – to as little stimulation as possible by censoring sexual images and references, and by keeping them as much in the dark and as much under a sense of prohibition as they can, they will thereby squeeze sex out of daily life, or at any rate keep it bottled.

But exactly there lies their mistake. Imprisoning sexual feel-ings is an invariable recipe for potentiating them. Ignorance about how to deal with them means that when they express themselves they might do so negatively, even harmfully – and with serious consequences: as when the combination of secrecy and shame with urgency results in couples not having con-traception available when they need it.

Moralists think they get everything they want by cementing sex to fertility, because pregnancy and child-rearing are well-known antaphrodisiacs, so the moralists can be confident that in most cases sexual passion between marital partners will diminish – although no sooner have moralists breathed a sigh of relief on that score than they find themselves deprecating the adultery and resulting family breakdown which frequently follow, without accepting the leading part their repressive views play.

What is the source of the moralists' strange idea that sex is wrong, bad, dirty, and in need of control? One answer is: the consequences of just such control – for if you dam a river it will flood elsewhere in awkward and unexpected ways. A major source of hostility to sex is religion. 'Christianity gave Eros poison to drink,' Nietzsche observed, 'but he did not die of it, he degenerated – into vice.' The belief that soul is heavenly and body earthly, and that everything earthly interferes with the soul's aspiration to heaven, is the fountainhead of negative evaluations of bodily things. Yet as Mark Twain said, 'Nature knows no indecencies; man invents them.'

That case is proved by the proliferation of sexually suggestive and explicit advertising. Some of it is tasteless – which is an aesthetic judgment, not a moral one – and some of it is beautiful and erotic. To the generous eye the latter adds delight and flavour to the world, while to the acidulated eye of prudery it is a lecherous and threatening affront. How sad, therefore, for the prude!

Prudery expresses itself most forcibly as censorship, and censorship has been at its most damaging, so far as the last century goes in the Anglophone world anyway, in relation to serious cinema. Until almost the end of the twentieth century, film censors in Britain – who were more liberal by far than those in America, but less liberal by far than those in the rest of Europe – generally left frank representation of sex to foreign-language cinema, doubtless because they thought that the alien provenance of such films gave a kind of zoological respectability to their sexual content. The censors also doubtless thought that since such films mainly attracted small audiences of intellectuals, their depiction of foreign goings-on would not damage the nation's morals at large.

By letting mainstream films with explicit sex scenes pass uncut (an important moment was the passing of the film-version of Hanif Kureishi's *Intimacy*), Britain's censors began to signal the crumbling of important taboos against public visual representation of such objects and activities as erect penises and oral sex. The significance of allowing these things to appear in mainstream cinema, rather than leaving them to the bracketed-off realm of pornography, is that it allows them to be incorporated more fully into debate about life's natural experiences. The best kinds of art include among their other purposes the encountering and exploration of what happens in ordinary life, and so long as certain things are kept out of view by obscenity laws and prudery, art is prevented from doing so – is prevented, in short, from telling the truth. Pornography cannot supply the lack, because its erections and oral sex are, among other merely repetitive frictions of body parts, the sole point; whereas in real life they are always a component of a larger and richer debate about love, needs, passions and sorrows, as real art almost always, and powerfully, shows.

But why are erect penises and oral sex taboo anyway? And when did they become so? Astonishingly, the removal from public view of erections and sexually various activities, relegating them to dark places of whispering and anxiety, is a very recent phenomenon, and one restricted almost exclusively to cultural traditions stemming from the 'religions of the Book' – Judaism, Christianity and Islam. Every other culture, historically and contemporaneously, which has escaped their attitudes to sex and the body has two notable features: a widespread celebration of sexuality in art and religion, and a complete absence of pornography (which is not, note, the same thing as erotica).

Thousands of pages could be filled in documentation of this claim. Look at the painted pottery of the classical world, and at its statuary, jewellery and murals. They are full of frank depictions of all forms of heterosexual and homosexual activity, and of celebration of the erect penis as a positive symbol. Women and girls standardly wore penis amulets as lucky charms, erections were carved over the doors of houses to bring good fortune, and sculpted priapic herms stood at rural crossroads to protect travellers.

The sources of this sexual celebration are deep and ancient. In Mesopotamia four thousand years ago the same word denoted 'semen' and 'fresh water', the connection lying in the power of both to fecundate. Survival depended upon the herds reproducing and the crops growing; all life turned on fertility, and death lay with its opposite, so it is scarcely surprising that sex and all that appertains to it should have been a matter of great interest and ubiquitous festival. Female fertility icons, from the magnificently plump and ample Venus of Willendorf onwards, remain familiar, but equally important male sexual iconography has almost disappeared from view.

The growth of civilisation is measured by refinements of living and increasing distance from the immediacies of survival. In matters of sex, the cultivation of physical pleasure for its own sake was a natural concomitant of this process, as the beautiful art of India, China and Japan illustrates. But this has never been so wherever the 'religions of the Book' have achieved dominance. Jewish sexual morality is the morality of herdsmen anxious to increase the number of their flocks and children. Its chief and overriding aim is reproduction. Therefore, although a man can easily divorce his wife, or take concubines, to ensure that he has offspring, he must not do anything that misdirects his seed from reproductive uses. Oral sex, homosexuality, and masturbation were thus rendered abominations. Onan, remember, was struck dead by God for not placing his seed in his dead brother's wife's womb.

Now add two unlucky accidents of Christian history. The first was the early Christian belief that the Second Coming was imminent, and that the faithful should therefore remain celibate. On these few words of St Paul rests a groaning mass of subsequent sexual frustration in Western history, and its inevitable result: pornography and deviation. When the Second Coming did not happen, Christianity was already in the hands of philosophers who found it a welcoming home for Plato's view that spirit is good and must be cultivated, whereas body is bad and must be disciplined. This is the second accident. The inevitable followed, from monasticism to the extremes represented by Origen castrating himself to escape his sexual longings.

Islamic art, for example in Mughal India, was once able to address love and its expression. Islam has since become as fiercely prudish as the worst kind of Christian puritanism. To think of erections and fellatio being publicly viewable in any traditionalist Islamic dispensation, is to think the impossible.

One signal effect of restrictive morality, at least as an official ethos, is that it provides men with ways to control women's sexuality and fertility. The historical result was the expectation of female virginity before marriage and chastity after it, with very severe penalties for non-compliance, thus ensuring that men were genuinely the fathers of the children to whom they bequeathed their property. Men, of course, were subject to the same constraints only in theory.

It was in particular Christian puritanism after the Reformation which added the final touch to Western attitudes to sex. Puritanism regards sex as an evil attendant on the expulsion from Eden. At its extreme it teaches that husbands and wives sin if they enjoy their conjugal duty to reproduce. The generalisation of this miasma of prudery spread in Europe from the seventeenth century until its apogee in the nineteenth. One of the illustrations of the folly it provoked is the British Museum's reputed decision to chip off penises on Greek statues in its possession, to save the blushes of its Victorian visitors. By one of the quirks of history, most of the penises on classical statues depicting male beauty are small, as a symbol of continence; the giant phalluses of satyrs and Priapuses are not meant to suggest

that erotomanes have big penises, but big appetites. By muti-
lating the statues, the prudes thereby obliterated classical
tokens of moral restraint.

Among the Malays who live in the Cape in South Africa it is
a sign of female beauty to have the four upper and lower front
teeth missing. This is allegedly because it facilitates fellatio,
the chief form of contraception in the community. As a cultural
mark of the centrality of sex in life, Malay orthodontics lie on
a continuum with the joyful statues of India's Konarak and
Khajuraho temples, and from them to the immense wealth
of erotic and passionate art in most non-Abrahamic cultures
beyond. If the censors' passing of frank content in serious
cinema means that the strangulated and distorted sexual attitudes of the West are thawing back to the human mainstream
at last, it is a welcome and grateful sign.

Just how much Britain's own recent cultural mainstream incorporated sexual frankness is demonstrated in an entertaining and
illuminating account by Ian Littlewood (called *Sultry Climates*)
of what the eighteenth-century Grand Tour was in large part
really about. Littlewood originally won his spurs by writing
literary companions to Paris and Venice, proving him to be a
discerning guide to intellectual and cultural landscapes. While
working on those books, he says, he noticed that alongside the
officially recorded responses of travellers there was a secret
history unfolding too, of travel to territories of experience closed
at home: territories of sexual encounter and awakening, of
freedom and felicity, of release and long-pent sensual expression.
For men and women both, travelling abroad always was (as it
still is) a journey to liberation, arriving sometimes at love but
often at sexual pleasure for its own sake.

Rich youths went on their eighteenth-century Grand Tours
ostensibly to acquire languages and politeness, culture, and an
insight into foreign ways, but in reality they acquired much of

a less mentionable nature besides – not just gambling debts but sexual experience and often enough the pox. Sexual experience was an aspect of the tour covertly welcomed by parents at home; Chesterfield said of his son that 'The Princess of Borghese was so kind as to put him a little upon his haunches, by putting him frequently upon her own. Nothing dresses a young fellow more than having been between such pillars, with an experienced mistress.' As Boswell's frank record shows, the different mores and morals of Abroad offered a wealth of opportunities for the repressed tourist to throw off his shackles, a fact which, once grasped, was never afterwards forgotten – and remains part of the motivation for clubbers heading to Ibiza and Shirley Valentines heading for Greece.

For convenience Littlewood classifies sexual travellers into connoisseurs, pilgrims and rebels. The first group comprises Grand Tourists, the second those Romantic seekers after self-discovery who expected (and often found) fulfilment in the holy places of antique culture, and the third those who travelled as a way of rejecting the restrictions of home. That this taxonomy is not exclusive is already implied in the idea that many in the first two categories also belonged to the third. A signal example of the rebel is afforded by Norman Douglas, who abandoned his diplomatic career when he discovered his homosexuality. Giving lunch to a visitor from England in a Florentine café, he pointed out a young waiter and described his charms in bed, and then asked, 'When are you coming out here to join us?' Douglas is the paradigm of the gay or bisexual man for whom escape from what he called the 'murk' of England – a moral and emotional murk – was release into life itself. Italy, North Africa, and between the two world wars Berlin, were havens for such, from Oscar Wilde and Andre Gide to Christopher Isherwood.

Central to Littlewood's account is the thesis that sex and travel have a basic affinity, as evidenced by our sexual vocabulary: 'roving eyes and wandering hands, exploring, mounting, entering, penetrating, riding, galloping, coming, going all the way'. And in another direction there is a link between travel and rebellion: 'The moment of illicit sexual satisfaction is a brief erotic victory over the rest of the world,' he writes, 'a successful raid on the kingdom of propriety.'

Although Littlewood's chief geographical focus is France and Italy, he makes an interesting foray to Polynesia because of its significance as a sexual Eden in literature and legend, which – from the *Bounty*'s mutineers to the idyll of Gauguin – riveted the attention and excited the longing of many. Imagine the amazement (and, among the po-faced, the horror) when news reached eighteenth-century England of a paradise where beautiful young girls swam naked to visiting ships, their long black hair streaming in the water behind them, offering themselves to the sailors in return for the gift of a single nail – so prized was iron among the Tahitians then. Hawkesworth and de Bougainville reported the ease, the sensuality, the laughing unconcern with which the lovely island girls gave their favours. Predictably, when Christian missionaries set to work in the South Seas, it was with a grim determination to stamp out this 'detestable licentiousness', a large part of their plan being to 'extirpate' the easily available bread-fruit from the islands so that their inhabitants would have to work for their food, thereby disciplining themselves 'in the sweat of their brows', leaving them far less time for misbehaviour.

Among the plethora of throwaway detail in Littlewood's story is his account of the cult of the sun that brought life to the French Riviera (which, until the 1920s, was closed in summer, for it was a wintering resort only). The writers and artists who discovered its glorious – and to begin with gloriously inexpensive – summers had themselves made the connection between hot weather and sex which we now think is too obvious and enjoyable to miss. The shedding of dress and the shedding of moral restraint go together in our frosted northern imaginations, showing, as Littlewood points out, that 'the central link between sex and travel is not to do with the meeting of bodies, but with the working of imagination.'

In discussing sex it is easy to confuse two separable though related things, namely, its psychological and biological aspects. Instructive treatises on these respective aspects are Geoffrey Miller's *The Mating Mind* and Tim Birkhead's *Promiscuity*. The first is about sex, the second is about reproduction. The one about sex is by a psychologist, the one about reproduction by a biologist. The one about sex, by psychologist Miller, talks of human nature and culture, art and morality, beauty and play-fulness. The one about reproduction, by biologist Birkhead, talks of sperm, oviducts, sacs, eggs, spiders and chickens. Yet both in their radically different ways offer much illumination about the same thing.

These two tomes differ also in how cheering they are. Miller's psychological account has an upbeat, cultural, intellectual message to offer, which in a nutshell is that language and intel-ligence – and all that go with them – are to humans what the tail is to the peacock, viz. sexual ornamentation, aimed at promoting its possessor's attractiveness, and thereby improving his or her chances of getting a mate. Birkhead's biological account is less upbeat. It is about the polyandrous behaviour of females of almost all species, meaning that they collect sperm from several males, and internally select the best of it by physio-logical means. Miller tells us that brainpower is sexy, which we always thought was partially true; Birkhead tells us that females of most species are promiscuous, which we always knew while convincingly pretending to believe that only males are so.

The brainpower-is-sexy view has generally been regarded as merely a partial truth because although some women indeed claim to find smart men attractive, the reverse is not noticeably true, and may even be noticeably false. Moreover, the attractiveness of brainpower has its limits: if dusty old dons, after reading Miller's book, think they are in for a run of luck, they are out of luck. Lots of girls prefer the bad boy who dropped out of school to the good boy who is still there swotting. This makes Miller's thesis look a bit optimistic (Miller is a don). Birkhead's thesis is at least frankly pessimistic, as it applies to humans: the message is that if a girl is minded to get pregnant, vows and values are not going to stand in the way of her getting the genetic wherewithal from other than her usual supplier, if she thinks it necessary.

Birkhead is concerned to show that standard models of sexual reproduction in nature have to be substantially revised in the direction of new theses about choice and competition in the mating game *after* insemination has taken place. The standard model regards most females in nature as typically monogamous and passive, although it allows that male gaudiness (and female dullness) – as for example in birds – is a function of the fact that females do the choosing in the first place, with males competing for their favours. Birkhead amasses a mountain of data from across the animal kingdom to show that females are anything but monogamous and passive, and that a significant part of their non-passivity is post-coital – both of Darwin's concepts of sexual selection, namely competition between males and choice by females, apply, Birkhead says, *in utero*.

Selection operates more intensely on males because of this competition, but it also means that males and females are in conflict too, for the male wishes to be the fertiliser of the female's eggs, and therefore seeks to prevent or limit her insemination by other males. Accordingly his sperm may carry chemicals that alter her behaviour, perhaps by making her unreceptive to further copulations. They can damage her, or even shorten her life. In return, females use the male as a source of supply, exchanging sexual favours for gifts of food, or absorbing the nutriments in his sperm, or even eating him during or after copulation, as with certain spiders and mantids.

Birkhead's thesis about interuterine sperm competition and selection by the female depends in the end on good experimental and observational evidence showing the processes in action. As Birkhead demonstrates in the case of the headline-catching claims about human 'sperm wars' put forward by Robin Baker and Mark Bellis, which critics claimed was based on shaky evidence and slack thinking, great care is needed in science, even when hypotheses are in the early stages of mooting, as is the case with Birkhead's own.

It is a little unfair to caricature Miller's claim as 'brainpower is sexy', although that is what in large part his central thesis comes down to. But quite a lot of his book is about breasts, buttocks, clitorises and orgasms too, and although of course some will immediately see their connection with art and culture, not all might. And indeed it is not clear that Miller does either, for in telling us (e.g.) that pert breasts and plump round buttocks are signals of female youth and fitness, and that male choice evolutionarily selected the favoured size and shape of these things not to mark maturity so much as to distinguish younger women from older less fertile women with flat drooping breasts and cellulite, he seems to be stating the obvious; but whether or not he is right, he has left the mind some way behind.

Miller is on better ground with art, morality, language and creativity, the four distinctive features of human beings that evolutionary biology allegedly cannot understand because they are expensive in energy and have no obvious survival value. Miller's place for them as ornaments and allures in the sexual scheme of things has plausibility, although it would be a mistake to be purely reductive about them, for it is equally obvious that, given the intelligence and curiosity humans possess (however and whyever evolved), much in art and the social nexuses of morality and language seems intrinsically and not merely instrumentally worthwhile – thus, most of us enjoy looking at paintings not because we think it will make us attractive, but because we enjoy looking at paintings.

On at least one point Miller is wholly persuasive: that the evolution of the *Homo sapiens* brain must have taken place by something like the rapid feedback mechanism he describes as a 'runaway process' in which given evolutionary adaptations take hold and become dominant. It is natural to think that the bigness of the human brain is causally linked to consciousness and language, and these in turn to art and morality; and it is further natural to think – if you accept a fundamental premise of all evolutionary theory, viz. that nature is economical and conservative, and never does anything without very good reason – that these adaptations must be *for* something useful.

But the economy assumption does not seem to be well founded. Only consider the billions of fish eggs that are released into the sea every day, a mere fraction of which become fishes. Nature seems immensely profligate and spendthrift. Nor is 'attractiveness to potential mates' the only plausible candidate for the reason why the adaptations of intelligence and language occurred – although it may well be one of them. These two doubts do not make Miller's entertaining thesis less persuasive, for he could be right; but even if he is, his view can only be part of the tale.

One thing is sure. If sexual activity were allowed its natural place in human life and society, it would very probably consume less time and energy than it now does. Sex occupies an absurdly inflated part of the moral horizon, and in many respects is surrounded by muddle and even misery. Prohibitions, anxieties, and what amounts to social rationing inflate the importance of sex ('the hungry individual thinks only of food'), and also in some cases distort it – for frustrated instincts are more prone to seek unusual, sometimes harmful, outlets than more easily satisfiable ones.

A kindly nature has made sexual activity pleasurable, not just to encourage reproduction but to promote bonding and, plausibly, health also. Our closest primate relatives, bonobo chimpanzees, enjoy frequent sexual encounters as a means of bonding and recreation, just as do humans. Among other primates mating activity is influenced by the oestrus cycle, which renders female sexual interest periodic. Otherwise chimpanzees, gorillas and ourangs do not moralise, still less agonise, about sex, but simply get on with it when occasion calls.

Matters are greatly more complex with humans, of course, and there is no clear answer to the question: what is the 'natural place' of sex in human life? A woman's potential investment in sexual activity, with its possible consequences of pregnancy, birth and child-care, is so heavy that it seems natural to expect her to be more selective about partners and more circumspect about engaging in sex, than is a man – at very least, when contraception is unavailable or unreliable. If some characteristic kinds of male homosexual activity are any guide to male sexuality in general, most or at least many men are rather like bonobo chimpanzees, in being apt – if offered the opportunity – to engage freely in frequent casual sexual encounters, attended by little emotional commitment. On this view, the argument might be that heterosexual males differ from their homosexual brothers only in having, as a rule, less opportunity for sex than they, owing to conventions and the restraints imposed by potential partners. (The dividing line between heterosexual and homosexual is by no means so definite as these remarks suggest; sharpening of the demarcation is a recent social artefact.)

It seems that if women's potential investment in sex is reduced by effective contraception and greater economic independence, their attitudes liberalise. In particular, wherever women attain equal status in business and the professions, their sexual behaviour comes increasingly to resemble that of men – even in such notable respects as, for example, employing prostitutes while on business trips (often female prostitutes, it seems), and in having more casual or opportunistic sexual encounters generally. (The similarities do not end there; it seems that increasingly many women business executives suffer stress-induced hair-loss.) And these points are independent of those reported above from Birkhead (and from Robin Baker and Mark Bellis) about reproductive promiscuity.

These points suggest that men and women differ in sexual behaviour only when the latter are obliged to be circumspect about consequences. The advance of science has made these factors contingent, not essential; anatomy is no longer destiny. So everything that needs to be said about sexual morality and liberation applies equally to both sexes.

Benevolence

Men always love what is good or what they find good; it is in judging of the good that they go wrong.

ROUSSEAU

Henry Fielding had a mixed press in his own century. Sir John Hawkins attacked his *Tom Jones* as a book 'seemingly intended to sap the foundation of that morality which it is the duty of parents and all public instructors to inculcate in the minds of young people', and Dr Johnson, despite his own tenderness for the bosoms visible in the dressing-rooms of Garrick's theatre, described it as 'vicious'. But Edward Gibbon, pointing out that Fielding was a scion of the English branch of the Habsburg family, claimed that long after the Emperors are forgotten, Fielding's work will live on.

The philosopher Bernard Harrison described Fielding's outlook as 'a morality of good heartedness'. This emotion is described by Fielding himself as 'that benevolent and amiable Temper of Mind which disposes us to feel the Misfortunes and enjoy the Happiness of others; and consequently pushes us on to promote the latter, and prevent the former; and that without any abstract Contemplation of the Beauty of Virtue, and without the Allurement or Terrors of Religion.'

The whole of *Tom Jones* is a demonstration of this rational, optimistic, and very Enlightenment principle. But Fielding's first and clearest statement of the idea occurs in the too-neglected work in which his comic genius found itself, and which, in the figure of Parson Adams, contains one of the most endearing characters in English literature: his novel *Joseph Andrews*.

Fielding wrote this novel as a satirical response to Samuel Richardson's best-seller *Pamela*. Richardson's tale is ostensibly one of virtue rewarded; serving-maid Pamela repulses the repeated libidinous assaults of her employer Squire B, and eventually he marries her. Fielding saw the book as a coyly drawn-out, sensationalist description of panting lust and near-rape, in which a determined tease in the end gets greater worldly rewards by inflaming passions than by yielding to them.

At first Fielding wrote a short and rather clumsy pamphlet, *Shamela*, to expose what he saw as Richardson's hypocrisy. As a way of improving and extending his treatment he invented Pamela's brother, Joseph, and subjected him to the same assaults, this time by Squire B's wife Lady Booby, and her companion Mrs Slipslop. The big difference is that Joseph has no intention of being disloyal to his beloved Fanny back home. His reward for virtue is more realistic than his sister's: first he is dismissed, and then attacked and stripped by robbers. From this plight he is rescued by Parson Adams, Squire Booby's curate. Here the adventure proper begins, as the two good men try to make their way home through an hilariously wicked world.

The guileless virtue of Parson Adams becomes the novel's fulcrum. Succouring the distressed, discussing the beauties of Homer's poetry, and punching a publican on the nose, come equally naturally to the parson, and Fielding extracts much high humour from his innocence of city ways, as evidenced by his mistaking a cure for venereal affliction as a form of spiritual retreat.

There is something strangely contemporary about some of Adams' encounters. Discussing charity with a rich fellow passenger who likes neither the word nor the idea, Adams says, 'Sir, my definition of charity is, a generous disposition to relieve the distressed', to which the other replies, 'Alas! Mr Adams, who are meant by the distressed? Believe me, the distresses of mankind are mostly imaginary, and it would be rather folly than goodness to relieve them,' to which he adds that no one can be hungry in a country 'where excellent salads are to be gathered in every field', and as for nakedness: well, clothes are no more necessary for man than for beasts. Adams, finding these remarks unbearable, leaps from the carriage without asking it to stop.

Once encountered, Parson Adams and his refreshing view of the world – and his propensity for getting into trouble and falling into ditches, ponds and other declivities because he is 'lost in contemplation of a passage in Aeschylus' – are unforgettable. So is the character of his moral outlook, and his instinctive readiness to act upon it.

Richardson and Fielding between them invented the English novel. The latter has the greater claim in this respect than Richardson, who adapted the epistolary technique for fictional purposes whereas Fielding blended the example of Cervantes with realism, psychological perceptiveness, and more complex structure. (The talent for burlesque of the third in the usual triumvirate, Smollett, has not weathered so well.) But it is Fielding's rich expression of an optimistic Enlightenment ethics that sets him apart, an outlook which, for all the comedy of its embodiment in Parson Adams, still offers one of the best hopes for civilising the world.

Morality

The great secret of morals is love.

SHELLEY

When Adolf Eichmann visited the death camp at Chelmno, where victims were gassed in sealed trucks, he found himself unable to watch the proceedings. 'I didn't stay to watch the whole manoeuvre. I couldn't stand the screams ... I fled. I jumped into the car and for a long time I couldn't open my mouth.' Later he attended a mass execution in Minsk. 'My knees turned to water,' he said, recalling how he had seen a woman throw her arms out behind her as she was shot. 'I had to leave.' He went to Auschwitz. 'I preferred not to watch the way they asphyxiated people ... They burned the corpses on a gigantic iron grille ... I couldn't stand it; I was overcome with nausea.' And Eichmann reports that he was not alone among high Nazi officials who responded in this way. Himmler visited a death camp to inspect it, and had to leave; 'he lost his nerve,' Eichmann says.

Remember who Eichmann was. He was the self-styled 'Jewish specialist' in charge of 'Gestapo Department IV B4 for Jewish Affairs', responsible for keeping the trains moving across all Europe to the death camps of the Final Solution. It is a ghastly fact that he could not bear personal witness to the mass murder he orchestrated. Grant that he was somehow incapable of imagining the vileness of it from the quiet of his office; why did he not, when he saw what it meant in reality, cry out in pity and horror, 'Stop it! No more!' He merely fled, and let it continue. What explains such moral perversion?

That is one of the questions posed by Tzvetan Todorov in his powerful book *Facing the Extreme: Moral Life in the Concentration Camps*. But it comes couched in a larger aim, which is to see the death camps of Nazism and the slave camps of the Soviet gulag as a magnifying mirror reflecting the moral character of man, in which one can see, with an often burning clarity etched by the extremity of the circumstances they imposed, the nature of good and evil. Primo Levi, writing of Auschwitz, said that 'fundamental values, even if they are not positive, can be deduced from this particular world', and Todorov takes the remark as his cue, examining the moral universe of the camps to bring central questions of morality more sharply into focus.

It is a commonplace that the degradation of life in the camps turned people into animals. Victims themselves said so. Tadeusz Borowski, who survived Auschwitz only to kill himself in 1951, said that war utterly abolishes notions of humanity; 'there is no crime a man will not commit to save himself'. In the same vein Levi wrote that the struggle to survive in the camps was 'without respite, because everyone was desperately and ferociously alone ... It was necessary to throttle all dignity and kill all conscience, to climb down into the arena as a beast against other beasts ... it was a war of everyone against everyone else.' The Hobbesian terror of this debased existence was the consequence of conscious design: the oppressors stripped their victims naked, left them to live in their own filth and excrement, starved them, turned them into competitors for scraps of food, denuded them of their names and identities. Under such treatment, in such extremity, how could the camps not be nightmares of hell, in which the very idea of morality loses all content?

And yet, as Todorov patiently and carefully shows, the reverse is true. In the camps there were acts of kindness, heroism, love and succour of the most moving kinds. Some reported that their personal philosophy for surviving the camps was 'me first, me second, me third – and then me again', as the physician Ena Weiss claimed, yet she herself spent every day helping others, at great personal cost. Robert Antelme, a survivor of Buchenwald, described a man and his son 'hungry together ... offering each other their bread with loving eyes.'

Todorov derives two theses from his examination of many accounts of camp life. The first is that survivors generally paint a bleaker picture of camp morality than the facts support. One reason is that they need to emphasise negative aspects of their experience because that is what made it unique; that is what specifies the absolute difference between camp experience and ordinary life. Another reason is that it expresses their remorse, even guilt, at escaping while so many others died.

The second thesis follows from the first. It is that the survival of moral life in the extreme horrors of the camps disproves the view that morality is a thin, conventional, easily dislodged veneer on human life. It shows instead that morality is natural, a firm property of human social existence, which can only be distorted or obliterated in very extreme circumstances. It takes beatings, terror, humiliation, imprisonment, starvation, cold, suffering, misery, loss of hope and identity, to root it out – and even then, it is not rooted out completely, or from everyone. That is a magnificently hopeful fact.

It confirms again what we all wish to believe: that moral heroism is no fiction, and that humans can cling to their humanity in the very worst of times, and survive.

Public Culture

Identity

If you cannot resolve what you are, at last you will be nothing.
MARTIAL

At first glance it might seem that the nations of Europe are culturally very diverse. Southern Europeans sip a glass of wine in the evening at a terrace café, northern Europeans drink jugs of beer in noisy pubs or beer gardens; the contrast seems emblematic, and it is not solely a matter of climate. Dress and diet, customs of social interaction, patterns of the working day, television entertainment, and much besides, differ in many ways throughout Europe independently of the rough north-south divide. The differences are very often a matter for celebration, as the pleasures of travel in Europe demonstrate; which justifies the quite proper desire most of us feel to see cultural diversity maintained.

But the diversity is by no means as great as some think, and in many respects is illusory. For one thing, elite culture – the enjoyment of music and the fine arts, appreciation of literature, exchange of ideas, research and collaboration in the sciences – is the same now as it always has been in Europe, with the difference that English has replaced Latin as the lingua franca of educated people. The community of interests and practices in elite culture explains why it is so natural for a German orchestra to appoint an Englishman as its conductor, or for

London's opera houses to be home to French and Italian stars. The explanation is not far to seek: it is that Europe shares a rich, continuous, vivid family of traditions in music, the arts and thought, so that any European, whether from Glasgow or Prague, Paris or Athens, entering an art gallery or concert hall in any other of these cities, will immediately feel at home; the assumptions and conceptual vocabulary of the entire framework of European tradition are the common point of reference.

The sharpest differences might therefore be supposed to lie at the demotic level. An alleged example is sense of humour. At a dinner party in Paris consisting largely of French architects and engineers with some English visitors, one of the company remarked that she was, in line of duty, about to spend a day touring Paris's grand sewers in a boat, and that therefore she was going to take a picnic for herself and companions. An English guest quipped, '*Dejeuner sur la merde, eh?*' The assembled French found this not in the least witty, and doubtless they were right. But it might have been the Englishman's pronunciation, or (implausibly) the other guests' ignorance of Manet's works, that scuppered things, and not a gulf in perceptions of funniness. The first option is probably right, for, after all, the British sitcom '*Allo 'Allo* is a hit in France, the Dutch watch hours of both British and German television, and the Germans translate scores of British publications every year – so even before one begins to think about football, pop music, and the fact that all Europeans welcome American fast-foods and cinema, one sees that there is more in common to the demotic cultures of Europe than superficial differences suggest.

None of this says that you cannot list, seemingly endlessly, the caricature differences among Europeans that charm or irritate. Each nation likes to distance itself, too; in highly inaccurate but self-congratulatory mode, the British like to think of themselves as phlegmatic and commonsensical, as against the existential airiness of the French. The caricatures do a disservice to the British poets and philosophers and the French mathematicians and scientists who have made their putatively non-national contributions to the flourishing of Europe's mind.

There is, in short, much that is misleading about the appearance of differences. Examples of the far deeper cultural familyhood of Europe abound as soon as deeper matters arise. Those who attend literary, scientific or educational conferences in various European locations invariably note that once the business in hand has commenced, the accidental fact that this speaker is from Germany or that from Italy is an irrelevance: the currency of ideas is entirely mutual; no one has to explain the cultural references that make the group members of one community. No one there, and no European in the ordinary course of conversation with another, would dream of explaining who Plato or Freud are, or of giving Goethe's full names in case he is mistaken for Jimmy Goethe from Hackney, or of saying 'the composer Beethoven'. Such facts reveal the depth to which the European cultural tradition is shared, and illustrate the truth that the very idea of differences only makes sense against a common background. Even the bitterness of Europe's wars is to be explained by closeness rather than distance in what is shared; it is a commonplace that enmities between brothers tend to be more violent than those between strangers.

Cultures

Culture is half-way to heaven.

GEORGE MEREDITH

Some years ago the literary theorist and Urdu poet Aijaz Ahmad engaged in a celebrated controversy with the American critic Frederic Jameson over the question of 'Third World Literature'. Jameson had eloquently advocated a widening of the literature syllabus in American academies to include works from outside the standard list of Western classics. Ahmad welcomed Jameson's call, but was deeply disturbed to find him talking of 'Third World Literature' as if it were an homogeneous category. There is, Ahmad argues, no such category: there are instead the many diverse literatures of many different countries which for reasons of geopolitical theory tend too glibly to be lumped together as 'the Third World'.

This observation is as true and profound as it is simple. In Ahmad's view, the 'metropolitan' (First World, Western) propensity to think in agglomerative terms of 'Third World Culture' generates a false understanding of recent world history and the way literature relates to it. The story goes as follows. In the three decades following 1945 nationalism was a powerful force in African and Asian countries engaged in throwing off colonial bonds. Literary theorists applauded the drive to cultural independence associated with these anti-colonial struggles; but in doing so they subsumed them all under the single 'Third World' label. But with the rise of post-structuralist literary theories in the 1970s nationalism itself came to be seen as oppressive, coercive, and retrograde. According to post-structuralism, it is nonsensical to think in terms of such concepts as the origin of national identity and the possession of collective cultural consciousness; and it is likewise mistaken to interpret the development of these phenomena by means of determinate historical narratives. There are only individual human beings, each – said the post-structuralists – with his own relative point of view; and they likewise argued that there is no independent rationality or historical truth by whose means sense can be made of national struggles and the fate of cultures.

Ahmad was opposed both to 'Third-Worldism' and to post-structuralism. His chief reason was that despite the fact that the political, economic and historical analyses offered by Marxism appear to have been exploded by events, he remained a Marxist nonetheless; and as such believes that although nationalism has too often suppressed questions of 'gender' and class, and has too often been retrogressive, it nevertheless has progressive forms, and these must be historically understood.

If fellow-critics try to dismiss Ahmad's views on the grounds that the moths of history have eaten his theoretical garb bare, they will be doing him an injustice. Marxist theory may be in eclipse, but on this occasion it serves as a powerful dissenting voice to the two orthodoxies – 'Third-Worldism' and post-structuralism – which have succeeded each other in misrepresenting, as Ahmad convincingly showed, the nature of the many different literatures and cultures flourishing in Africa and Asia.

One of the best features of Ahmad's view is its disentangling of geopolitical appearances from cultural realities. At the Bandung Conference in Indonesia in 1955, presided over by the formidable figures of Nehru and Zhou En Lai, an effort was made to forge a consensus among nations outside the immediate hegemonies of the United States and Soviet Union. Writers like Edward Said have mythologised this moment as the birth of the Third World; but Ahmad showed that for all its importance otherwise, Bandung does not mark – for nothing could ever mark – the creation of that 'Third World Culture' which metropolitan criticism, addressing itself to a phantom of its own making, so vociferously praised and then later so vehemently attacked.

There are even more general points to be made about 'cultural politics'. Despite appearances in the absurd and often comic debate about 'political correctness', the concept of high culture is not the possession of the political Right, nor does rejection of 'post-modernism' and its essence, relativism (rejection of which is required for defence not just of the notion but of the value of high culture), amount to rejection of a progressive political perspective. Political resistance against hegemonies of wealth, class, race and sex in the late-twentieth-century Western world has mistakenly included rejection of the idea that there are cultural and intellectual values which transcend accidental boundaries in human experience, and thereby constitute a possession for the species as a whole. It has been a cheap source of reputation for 'theorists' to claim that 'reality is the product of discourse', which means that different discourses constitute different realities, and therefore that truth and value are relative. Those who mistake the politics of resentment for the politics of justice find such views useful, because they equate 'high culture' with 'culture of the politically and economically dominant class, race or sex', and therefore take it that attacks on the former are attacks on the latter. One disastrous consequence is that it allows the political Right to present itself as the defender of art, literature and free intellectual speculation, whereas historically it has been the Right – from Plato onwards – which has sought to repress the best human endeavours in these respects, on the grounds that art, literature and the unrestricted play of reason threaten to set people free and to make them equal.

Rather than attacking the idea of high culture, therefore, reflective progressives (that is or should be a pleonasm) should assert their right to the high cultural terrain, and disentangle themselves from those aspects of movements, particularly in ethnic and sexual politics, whose tendency is not to promote the realisation of a just society, but satisfaction of the petty appetite for revenge on groups perceived as historical oppressors. A better aim for progressives would be to free high culture from the citadel of inaccessibility – mainly financial – into which dominant groups have kidnapped it. They should not commit all their attention to promoting counter-culture or 'mass' culture, for the excellent reason that – especially in respect of this latter – much of what passes for 'mass' culture is a means of manipulating majorities into quiescence and uncritical acceptance of political and economic conditions favourable to dominant groups. This is notably the case with escapist entertainment and sport. Luckily, it is not the case with certain kinds of comedy, nor with soap operas, both of which are sometimes as revealing of human truth as any other form of high-quality commentary and narrative.

Conservation

How the past perishes is how the future becomes.
ALFRED NORTH WHITEHEAD

Jeremy Bentham, the great utilitarian, was a man who practised what he preached. He owned a pair of houses in York Street, Westminster, and sensibly lived in one while renting out the other. The other happened to be the house where Milton once lived. Bentham let it to his colleague James Mill, whose son John Stuart Mill passed the early years of his life there, studying Greek and Latin under his father's eager tutelage – to the point where he nearly lost his mind. When the elder Mill quitted the house complaining of its darkness and damp, it was leased to the great essayist William Hazlitt, who lived there from 1812 to 1820, in which latter year Bentham evicted him for non-payment of rent.

Bentham was not in the slightest interested in the literary associations of his next-door property. At various times he contemplated demolishing it to enlarge his garden. In the end Westminster City Council, as utilitarian in its practices as Bentham himself, knocked down both the Milton-Mill-Hazlitt house and Bentham's own. It is natural to think that the nineteenth century was not squeamish about destroying iconic places in the way that we are now, and that Bentham's attitude was typical of its time. But matters were not so simple. Hazlitt was acutely aware of the risk of historical Luddism posed by Bentham towards his house – which he honoured as Milton's house, unchanged since Milton's time – and he was appalled by Bentham's attitude. Bentham's and Hazlitt's opposing views have since come to be the staple of the debate about conservation, a debate which in their day did not take the form, or have the urgency, that it now does, only because the rate of change was then slower, and far more of the past was present.

The Bentham view was long the orthodoxy, and it scarcely seemed to need arguing. It is a mistake, it says, to hang on to the past merely because it is past. Things – buildings, paintings, old furniture – have their lifespans as humans do, and when they get old and broken, dirty and inconvenient, decrepit and even dangerous, we should let them go. The past becomes a burden if we have too much piety towards it. Salvaging some things merely because they have existed for longer than other things is an inhibition to progress and a barrier to new ideas and fresh ways. The older things get, the more that current resources are needed to prop them up, to repair them and keep them safe. The past might live in the present, in the sense that old things might still be used and enjoyed; but as soon as they become mummies or museum items, they are merely baggage.

This view incorporates several strands. It attacks the physical and financial burden, generally an increasing one, of keeping old things in being. It attacks the psychological burden of being wedded to the past and thereby inhibited from innovating. It attacks historical pietism as a disguised form of timidity, always a major element in conservative attitudes. And it makes the good point that things, like people, have natural lifespans, and that unless we move forward we sink – look at China from the Song dynasty (which began in AD 960) to the Qing dynasty (which ended in 1911) as a prime example of almost complete entrapment and stultification in tradition (except for ceramics and prose literature).

Holders of the opposing view say that without respect for the past and understanding of it, we are blind and deaf to the present. Maintaining access to the past in the form of traditions, buildings, works of art, and places of special association, gives us a far richer and deeper insight into our route hither through time, and therefore into ourselves now and our possibilities for the future, than if we had lost all palpable trace of it. For example: a written or even photographic record of the remains of the Rose Theatre at Bankside – built in the early 1590s before the Globe, and the scene of Marlowe's triumphs and Shakespeare's beginnings – could not compare to the impact, both emotional and educational, of seeing that tiny space in its polygonal footings, with its sloping clay pit-floor and the foundations of the stage, and knowing that this was the very place, and these the very things, that saw the birth of all that wealth.

And even when the meanings of our present culture are not so vividly linked to the past in this way – even when the past is remoter, more silent, seemingly unconnected with the present, as with Stonehenge ('that huge, dumb heap, that stands on the blasted heath, and looks like a group of giants, bewildered, not knowing what to do, encumbering the earth, and turned to stone, while in the act of warring on Heaven') – we would be committing a sacrilege against our present selves if we bulldozed it to make way for a council estate. The very suggestion sends a chill: and it repays investigating why.

The march of the twentieth century, a blitzed, bombed and murderous epoch in which many of the cities of Europe – London, Berlin, Dresden, Warsaw – were subjected to massive physical destruction, and in which not only buildings but tens of thousands of artworks and archives were lost, saw a corresponding growth of official historical consciousness, as if in compensation. (This leaves out of account, for present purposes, the infinitely greater matter of the suffering of those who lived in these cities.) It has got to such a point that it now seems to critics as if far too many things, in apparently indiscriminate profusion, are listed, protected and preserved. An egregious example often cited is the rebuilding of the old centre of Warsaw – *'dov'era, com'era'*, as was said of the collapsed campanile of Venice: 'where it was, as it was' – as an exact replica of its former self. Walking through it makes one uncomfortable; it is ersatz, and feels like a mistaken gesture, a refusal to face facts and move on. The anxiety to preserve and even thus to recreate 'heritage' has, say critics, gone too far, inviting all the strictures of the Benthamite view.

But Warsaw is actually an unusual case, and its purpose was more a matter of psychology than historicism. Its gutted heart was a deep and savage wound, and rebuilding it was medicinal, restoring landmarks as homecoming beacons after a terrible disorientation. Few other places followed suit. In London, as the famous Surveys of London showed, a quiet sigh of relief went up when the City, the East End and the areas of South London close to the Thames were opened for renovation by the Luftwaffe. There had been precious little of value there. The City itself is an architectural palimpsest, constantly being rebuilt, an expensive throw-away region very short on real treasures – except those the mind sees, walking streets that are metres deep in historical meaning. New office blocks in the City have a projected life of a few decades only, and with rare exceptions their design is as utilitarian as Bentham could wish, at most involving a few cosmetic gestures. The opposite of conservation is built-in ephemerality; the City is not for conserving – is not for History, but Economics – and as in its investment practices, it is interested only in the short term.

It happens that conservation is no longer purely a matter of sentiment or intellectual commitment. Heritage is a major source of tourist revenue, and if Bentham had realised that he could charge a penny a time for visitors to troop through the house where Milton dictated Foreign Office missives in Latin, and Hazlitt scribbled notes for his essays on the wainscoting, the best utilitarian principles would have galvanised him into sprucing up the place and conserving it tenderly. One of the chief safeguards of the past is thus the fact that it has become a leisure resource. But that applies only to obvious things, such as cathedrals and castles, and places of literary association such as the houses of Dr Johnson and the Brontës. There is much of interest and value lying off the tourist track: stone-age hill forts, barrows and mounds, Roman pavements, the multiple strata of archaeology underpacking London; and more recent items such as the Lloyds building, Battersea power-station, and the Angel of the North. If the debate about conservation has a bite, it relates to these things.

Thinking about a choice between Stonehenge and a council estate focuses the mind on one clear point. It is that it is better to err on the side of preserving, because if one makes a mistake in so doing, it is remediable, whereas post-facto regret is no remedy. Current policy on historical conservation thus makes the right error. And it is not even clear that it is an error: after all, the majority of planning applications in respect of historical sites in Europe are granted, and for all the criticism they receive, heritage bodies in this history-rich geographical palimpsest appear to be conscious, in their practice as in their stated policy, that the past competes with the present and future, and that they deserve equal if not more consideration.

A healthy attitude towards conservation combines a sense of the strength of Hazlitt's side of the argument with a robust scepticism about why so many tithe barns and Georgian terraces have to be fenced off from progress. If time and leisure permitted, every candidate for conservation or restoration would be examined on its merits, and if kept would be properly kept, at the same time being integrated into the life of the present as far as is practicable. But time and leisure do not permit, which is why one needs principles and policies. Current policies – erring properly on the side of caution – are good. The principles are that things good of their kind are worth keeping for their own sake, and that there are also things worth keeping for the sake of understanding the past and therefore the present. The principles justify the policies.

Teachers

*A teacher affects eternity; he can never tell where his influence
stops.*

HENRY ADAMS

No doubt few parents would agree with Aristotle's view
that 'teachers should be more honoured than parents, for
whereas parents give their children life, teachers give their
children a good life.' Aristotle's thought is that to live well and
flourishingly, a person needs to be educated – which means:
informed, and able to think. He is of course right. But objecting
parents might point out that their contribution is not restricted
to merely biological duties, for they are teachers too; and moreover providers, carers, protectors and custodians – twenty-four
hours a day, seven days a week, for decades.

Aristotle's belief that teachers should be honoured is nevertheless apposite in light of the fact that teaching has never
been a highly paid profession – an extraordinary fact, given its
importance – but it was once a highly respected one, and the
status enjoyed by teachers helped compensate them for the
dedication and difficulty involved in their vocation. For vocation it is; no one who has chosen teaching over some other
occupation on merely pragmatic grounds has been able to stick
it, unless they fell in love with it – with the pleasure of youthful
company, and the satisfaction of seeing minds grow, understanding develop, and capabilities increase.

Part of the problem facing teaching in the contemporary world is that its status as a profession has been undermined by the contemptible view that only what makes money is admirable. When people lose sight of the invisible rewards on offer in different avocations, many kinds of work that make the world a better place suffer a loss of talent. No one denies that money is important too – it is the means to many satisfactions, not a few of them greatly worth having; and there is no reason why people who provide valuable services in teaching, medicine and other socially pivotal occupations, should be expected to do so at a discount. *Digna canis pabulo*, after all; the labourer is worthy of his hire. But in a social climate where invisible wages are considered beneath mention because beneath contempt, the danger is that good minds and hearts will be lost to honourable vocations, and people will jostle instead to be employed where pay-packets are largest and effort least.

Intellectuals

An intellectual is someone whose mind watches itself.

CAMUS

Scourers of second-hand bookshops, who collect books to read rather than merely to collect, and who delight in those dusty Bohn's Library and Everyman editions which contain everything and more of the past's literary treasures, will be familiar with the experience of finding volumes annotated by earlier readers – frequently in ink, and often in beautiful clerkly hands – in which words have been underlined and their dictionary definitions entered alongside, and with names, likewise emphasised, earnestly supplied with one-sentence biographies in the margins.

In a collection of Addison's essays on the desk beside me as I write there are many examples of this studious autodidacticism. I look at random and find the name 'Ben Jonson' underlined in blue ink with the help of a ruler, and in the margin a laborious hand has written, 'Playwright and poet 1572–1637 AD.' It is a touching vision; it makes one think of the medieval tanner's son, one of a family so numerous and poor that they could not afford a candle, and who therefore, after a day's long labour, took his book to the church so that he could read under its porch lantern. The boy grew up to become a scholar and teacher, and one might say the patron saint of all those people, invariably from among the poor, who discovered books and taught themselves; a numerous, noble, heroic army of men and women, who by their own efforts conquered more than any general has ever done: the fortifications at the foot of Parnassus.

The high moment of this epic is the nineteenth and early twentieth centuries, and its story is a fascinating one. Anyone who disdains the educational opportunities now abundantly on offer in the contemporary West should enquire about this period in intellectual history (should indeed be made to do so) because it illustrates how human intelligence, however oppressed, can slake its thirst for knowledge – or more accurately, since this is the true goal beyond knowledge: for understanding – if given half a chance.

What is striking about the variety of autodidact experiences which flowed from the Victorian spread of general education, and the concomitant proliferation of public libraries, is how often the beneficiaries of both produced eloquent and elegiac accounts of the excitement which books – and not just books, but music, theatre, opera, all the delights of high culture – prompted in them. The children of well-off parents, with educational opportunities commensurate with the home environments from which so much cultural familiarity is absorbed, can be denied the extraordinary delight felt by the self-taught man first stumbling across Ruskin or Marx, Beethoven or Rembrandt. A clue lies in this to the reason why these things matter more than the artefacts of the commonplace; one imagines the eager, darting look of an intelligent eye, unblinkered by conventional education, seeing the value in things without having been told to expect them there – and therefore seeing them truly.

Ruskin is one of the salient names in this story. He figures at the top of the list of influences for MPs in the early Labour Party, almost all of them men from working-class backgrounds whose educations were substantially, if not wholly, self-provided. An Oldham millworker who became Lord Privy Seal,

J. R. Clynes, encountered Ruskin when young, having bought *The Seven Lamps of Architecture* for a shilling he could ill afford. 'For many weeks,' Clynes later wrote, 'I read and re-read this one book, and so illumining was the love I held for it that, before I had perused it the third time, its every subtlety of meaning was as much my own intimate possession as a young lover's memory of his virgin kiss.'

It did not matter that the subject of that particular book was architecture. One book led to another, breeding a consciousness of debate, of ideas unfolding into further ideas, inviting agreement or controversy, raising questions which further books were needed to answer. When the Bible was the only book people knew, they naturally thought it embodied all that is true; but when their reading expanded, and with it the world, and a sense of other times, other voices, other possibilities and points of view, that authority could not last. By this means working people learned of their oppression and their rights, and formulated new hopes therefore. Women learned about their own bodies, and how to control their fertility. A worker in the Swindon railway factory taught himself Greek and Latin and thereafter published translations of Ovid, Pindar, Sappho, Plato, Menander and Horace; this was Alfred Williams. The tramp-poet W. H. Davies could only afford classics sold at second-hand bookstalls, so he had never read contemporary poetry, and when he met other poets he felt mildly embarrassed because they knew his work but he did not know theirs.

And so the stories go on – extraordinary and heartening, sometimes astonishing, often moving. Of course these autodidacts were a minority in their own class, and they more often suffered the disappointments of Jude Fawley in *Jude the Obscure* or the rebuffs of Leonard Bast in *Howard's End* than the successes of Williams and Davies. Bast's haunting fate is illustrative of the terrible snobbery too often encountered by working-class autodidacts. Bast – a bastard in cultural terms, straining to acquire culture, working hard at going to concerts and reading systematically, eventually killed by his own bookcase falling and crushing him – is the target of the uneasy, guilty disdain which (so some cultural commentators argue) led to modernism's attempts to lock the fortifications of Parnassus again, to keep out book-devouring workers and evening-class graduates by making culture too remote and difficult for them. On this view, access to modernist art and literature required the in-crowd knowingness of those already in possession of Parnassus's keys; so all the Bohn's Library and Everyman Classics in the world were no good to the factory hand who exchanged his luxurious shilling for them, or the dress-maker's assistant who bought a ticket for the gods at Covent Garden.

After 1945 the culture of self-education rapidly declined, partly because of increased formal schooling, partly because of television and other distractions, and partly because increasingly rapid changes in cultural fashion make self-taught classicism look conservative. No doubt the internet will spawn a new, perhaps a better, resource for autodidacts. But it will not be the same.

Community and Society

Politics

The punishment we suffer, if we refuse to take an interest in matters of government, is to live under the government of worse men.

PLATO

Politics and government are very different things. They interact, especially at election time, and almost everyone fails to see the difference – even, sometimes, politicians themselves, especially those in opposition, who are able to make promises proportional in size to the unlikelihood of their ever having to be fulfilled. But most responsible politicians recognise the difference between managing the complexities of a large and populous country, and the political endeavour of persuading voters to continue giving their support.

The public see only part of the external face of government. Its ordinary tasks, even those that are done well, rarely find mention in the media, which is hungry for mistakes, problems, lies, evasions, difficulties, conflicts, quarrels, arguments, disasters, miscalculations, personality clashes, and anything else which makes a good story. In consequence the public gets a low impression of politicians. Most politicians are indeed temporisers and opportunists, being either natural-born second-hand car-salesmen, which is why they chose politics in the first place, or having been made that way by the gruelling and pitiless dog-eat-dog character of the political life. Yet even if, improbably, there were not one single well-intentioned politician in the land, there are two connected things which in the end constrain those who conduct the government: freedom of the press, and the final sanction of the ballot.

If the press is free to seek and exploit the quarrels, difficulties, etc. just mentioned, it is by the same token and sometimes in the same breath able to expose genuine problems. The press indeed justifies its eagle-eyed watch for fissures, frictions and faults in both government and opposition by appeal to its performance of this democratic service. It often enough goes too far, conjuring mountains from molehills (or from nothing), but excess is better than deficit in this instance, because unless the press were absolutely vigilant, the politicians would use their time-honoured methods – cover-up, sleight of hand, rationalisation – to get away with things. They would think themselves foolish not to.

In consequence, consumers of the media have to exercise their own watchfulness. They have to exercise judgement concerning whether the media are offering a good story or a good point. They also have to balance what they read and hear of political strife with some acknowledgement of the difficulties of running a complicated society in which there are many conflicting interests, and many deserving claims which cannot all be met simultaneously. The easiest thing in the world is to complain from the sidelines; and so unforgiving is the stance of complaint that those on the pitch, *in medias res*, get scarcely any quarter, still less credit. 'It is very easy to accuse a government of imperfection,' Montaigne observed, 'for all mortal things are full of it.'

The importance of politics to government lies in the spirit, the aspiration, which would-be governors claim they will bring to the task of governing. That is what electors choose between: different visions of how the vast laborious machine will be geared and run, and what directions it will be pointed in, if turning it is a possibility. Genuine differences ensue, because small touches of change at the centre, radiating out into the lives of real individuals, have big effects. One can judge between candidates by remembering Georges Pompidou's remark that a statesman is a politician who puts himself at his country's service, whereas a politician is a statesman who puts the country at his own service – or that of a group or class, usually his own.

Among the worst of those who fail to distinguish between politics and government are those who proudly proclaim their determination not to vote. Most such do so on the grounds of entirely spurious analogies ('If two disagreeable boys asked me out, why should I be obliged to accept one of them?'), and all fail to recognise that their abstention might in effect work as a positive vote for the most disagreeable of the two boys. Not much nous is required to see why, but at election time, it seems, that is a commodity in shorter supply than usual.

Voting

Nobody will ever deprive the American people of the right to vote except the American people themselves — and the only way they can do that is by not voting.

FRANKLIN D. ROOSEVELT

A major theme in American and British elections at the turn of the twenty-first century was the question of voter turnout. It is remarkable that in countries which pride themselves on their democratic credentials, as these two do, there should be problems with turnout – especially in the United States, where fewer than half of those entitled to vote do so. In fact it is not so much remarkable as a scandal, given the often bloody strivings by which the right to vote was wrested from history – and given the fact that the contemporary world, for example in China and Burma, gave examples of the brave and bitter struggle for democracy.

It is said that unless you make a person pay for the advice you offer, he will not heed it. By the same token, if you give people democratic rights as a free entitlement of citizenship, they appear to disregard it, failing to see how precious and important it is. Memory cannot be so short that people have forgotten the long, hot but happy lines of newly enfranchised South Africans queuing all day to cast their vote in the first-ever proper elections in their country, when Apartheid had at last been overthrown.

The reason that so many are so neglectful of their democratic privileges is that they know no history. They do not realise how recently such privileges were won on their behalf, and at what cost. They do not, for example, connect their own freedom to vote with the excoriating image of the lone white-shirted demonstrator blocking a line of tanks in Beijing in 1989. If they grasped these points they would not be so cavalier and irresponsible about their democratic duties.

The United Kingdom achieved universal adult suffrage in 1929, when women were at last allowed to vote on equal terms with men. France attained the same democratic heights in 1944. When blacks were enfranchised in the United States in the 1960s, that great bastion of democracy – where all men are born equal – at last itself became democratic. These amazingly recent achievements were built on dead bodies. For centuries ordinary people struggled against absolute monarchs, rich aristocrats, princely bishops, colonisers, landowners and industrial magnates for a say in the running of their own lives. They did it on barricades, in demonstrations charged by sabre-wielding mounted cavalry, in sit-ins crushed by tanks. These people are dishonoured by stay-at-homes on polling day.

The required solution is that voting should be compulsory. One has to respect civil liberty arguments to the contrary, but the fact remains that citizenship imposes duties, many of them (such as paying taxes) already embodied in laws requiring observance on pain of sanctions. There are few more important matters than electing a government. Dissenters from the process can spoil their ballots as a way of abstaining, or can pay the fine if the walk to the booth is too much effort; or if they really wish to live somewhere that exempts them from democratic responsibilities, they could emigrate to Burma or China and see how they like it.

Sceptics and idlers think that their one vote will make no difference either way. They are wrong – wrong both in practice: some elections turn on mere handfuls of votes, as witness Al

Gore's fate in Florida – and in principle: for every refusal to vote is an act of self disenfranchisement in which a citizen, betraying the endeavours of history, demotes himself into a serf.

Utopia

Anyone who has ever built a New Heaven first found the power thereto in his own hell.

NIETZSCHE

In Oscar Wilde's view, everyone's mental map of the world should include a Utopia, because progress consists in arriving there and then seeing even better places to aspire to beyond. He thereby implies that Utopia is a good place. But 'utopia' strictly means 'nowhere', and has only come to mean a paradise of sorts as a result of assimilating its first syllable to the 'eu' of such words as 'euphoria', for 'eu' is a Greek prefix meaning 'good'. An antonym has therefore been invented – 'dystopia' – meaning a bad place. Some dystopias were not meant to be so – Huxley's brave new world and the 1984 of Orwell are chief examples of intentionally bad utopias, whereas the racially pure and healthy bucolic paradise envisaged by Hitler succeeds in being the same unintentionally – as does Plato's no less eugenic and authoritarian Republic.

But most utopias are offered by their inventors as eutopias, and they fall into two readily identifiable sorts. In doing so they comment on the condition of mankind; from the paradises dreamed by the utopiasts one can discern, as their reverse image, the too-familiar dystopian features of the world we live in. The majority sort of utopia is a land of unfailingly good weather – usually warm springtime – where there is a natural abundance of foodstuffs that has only to be plucked from the bough. Money does not exist, and in its absence there is neither greed nor strife, nor inequality of rank or station. Reason is governor, and sex is freely available. If there are criminals, they are treated as merely diseased, and sent somewhere pleasant to be cured. People are generally vegetarian in diet, and wear beautiful home-spun clothing. Either there is no machinery to despoil the natural environment, or it exists so that humans can be free to cultivate painting, knitting, calligraphy, or other gentle arts and crafts.

The minority sort of utopia is more austere, and is generally written by formidable feminist ladies. Sex has ceased to exist; utopia is all-female, whose occupants reproduce by partheno-genesis, and who stay wrinkle-free as a result of injections of animal extracts (secured under conditions exceedingly pleasant for the animals). When the accidental discoverers of these utopias are pleasant young men, they of course fall in love with one of the female residents, only to be discomfited or even expelled when their dystopic instincts collide with the new order. [These characterisations are distillations of Utopian imaginings entertainingly collected in *The Oxford Book of Uptopias* and other sources.]

It is scarcely remarkable that, over generations of writers, the dream of a better world should focus so sharply on remedies for inequality, poverty, hardship, labour, cold, and sexual privation. Yet seeing writer after writer paint a paradise exactly opposite to these realities of common life is very poignant, not least when it occurs to us that the few who occupy the top of the food-chain in human society suffer none of those pains, because they have the key – wealth – which unlocks the gates to a private version of that very dispensation. It is accordingly also unsurprising that some utopias envisage harsh remedies against those who have kept the masses in subjection so that they alone benefit. If anything is surprising, it is that centuries –

millenniums – of dreams of a fairer and easier world have still to come (or be made) true.

There have always been utopian visions, starting with the accounts of a past Golden Age in Hesiod and Homer. People soon saw how depressing and counter-productive it is to put utopia unreachably in the past, so they turned their attention to the future or to alternatives to the present. Plato gave us his vision of a rational society in the displeasing aristocratic Republic where only the best can breed and where the resulting children are raised in state nurseries. Tacitus later attempted to encourage his fellow Romans to return to Republican austerities by praising Rome's foes, the hardy warlike German tribes, who had 'never weakened themselves by intermarriage with foreigners'. Christian writers anticipated the pleasure of watching non-Christians burn agonisingly to death on Judgement Day (Tertullian especially smacked his lips at the thought), and Tao Qian in early China voiced a national theme in dreaming of peace and plenty in perpetual spring, untroubled by war or public duties.

And so the litany of dreams proceeds, taking their colour from their period and its concerns. The beginning of modern times in Europe – the seventeenth and eighteenth centuries – abounds in utopias fed by the promise of science, or by the discovery of allegedly noble savages whose simple life and upright dealings were offered to the powdered-wigged, patched-faced effete of Europe as a moral lesson. Dickens, writing after much Noble Savage propaganda had been generated by disaffected moralists, was exceedingly witty at the expense of savages, but alas in an entirely un-Politically Correct fashion.

In our own times utopias seem to have turned bleak and threatening. Technology has grown too much for us, and some of the horrors that earlier utopiasts sought to avoid in their paradises – not least among them over-population – have come to determine the picture of a violent and strife-torn planet where machines extend the savagery of man almost beyond imagining. If one were to plot on a graph the change from retrospective visions of Golden Ages to contemporary anticipations of Gehennas, the curve would run counter to the curve of technological development. The big cross thus made seems to state a moral.

Of all the utopias offered in world literature, only a few have had attempted actualisations, and only two of them concretely so: communism of the Marxist–Leninist inspiration, and the Garden City ideas of Ebenezer Howard. The former proved a hideous disaster, and still proves so in China. The latter have had more rather than less pleasant outcomes in the garden cities and suburbs of England and elsewhere in the world, and make one feel – with a certain surprise and hope – that there are species of utopianism that might after all make a positive difference.

Profit

A profit basely made is the same as a loss.

If you perform a service or produce a commodity for others, you should be rewarded for your pains. So much is only fair and right. If you do it well you deserve to be rewarded well; you deserve to profit by it. There is nothing in itself wrong with profit, nor with wealth, nor with any individual or company or country growing rich. Profit is an enabler, because it takes people and peoples beyond subsistence levels to the amenities of life, to comfort and culture, to new knowledge and new possibilities.

But wrong enters the picture when profits are made out of others' loss or suffering. That, alas, happens so often that it almost seems the norm.

It seems, at time of writing, that a certain well-known oil company makes more than £300 profit every second. This is an amazing and, to many, unappealing fact. Even so, it is not as disquieting as the fact that the chairman of a City company can earn in a year as much as fifty or a hundred nurses do. Why is that so? Defenders of high-flying businessmen point out that they have responsible jobs, producing wealth which, indirectly through taxation, helps pay nurses' wages. But is the chairman of a business worth fifty nurses? Indeed, is he worth one? The same, with even more of a barb, might be asked about football players and pop stars.

But even footballers' and businessmen's salary levels are not as disquieting as the fact that announcements about medical discoveries, for example in human genome research, are typically muddied because many of the laboratories involved, being owned or funded by private companies, are obliged to turn what they know into a cash profit. There is no mystery about why it is wrong that such a motive should interfere in the quest for fundamental knowledge about mankind. Understanding the human genome is, without question, one of the greatest and most important scientific advances in all history, and it promises treasures of understanding that will benefit every present and future individual. Private researchers ask us to buy, at a premium, vital knowledge about ourselves. How can that be acceptable?

Worse still, but in more complicated ways, is the fact that millions of Third-World people suffer and die because giant pharmaceutical companies sustain the prices of their drugs at developed-world levels. To critics this is an horrific example of the evil men do in the name of profit. Public outcry makes it appear so intolerable that even some of the large investors in pharmaceutical companies have begun to question the ethics of their behaviour. But the complication is that whereas it is unequivocally wrong that people in need of medicines cannot get them because of their cost, it is too simple to say that the pharmaceutical companies should turn into charities.

The reason is well known: developing new drugs is fabulously costly in money and time, made more so by the safety controls required by law; and it is risky, because a half-billion-dollar development programme might lead to nothing. To cover themselves the pharmaceutical companies have to charge whatever the market will bear, and protect their patents.

If the pharmaceutical companies did not exist, neither would the medications they develop. How is the tension between commercial considerations and human health to be resolved? Since the need to help the sick in developing countries is urgent, and because it is unrealistic and self-defeating to expect the pharmaceuticals to turn into charities, logic dictates the simple and obvious alternative: that the people and governments of the first world should buy the medications needed by sufferers in the third world, and give it to them.

The next question is: why do the simple and obvious alternatives turn out to be so complicated and so full of hidden difficulty – something which becomes apparent, mysteriously, just when the time comes to put our hands in our pockets to pay for them?

Power

The greater the power, the more dangerous the abuse.
EDMUND BURKE

Everyone knows Acton's saying about the corrupting power of power. History proves the truth of his observation by offering egregious individual examples, from Nero to Genghis Khan, from Tshaka the Zulu to Pol Pot. What is remarkable is how often power in the hands of an unconstrained individual or claque leads to harm. How many examples are there of the powerful reversing the world's entropic tendencies in order to bring peace, succour and comfort to those in need of them? Woefully few. It is a curious and unhappy fact that those who strive to provide these things – aid organisations, charities, individuals prompted into action by sympathy for the suffering of their fellows – tend themselves to be anything but powerful.

There are plenty of examples of harmful power in the contemporary world. Attention naturally fixes on dictators as cases of men resolved to get their own way, no matter what. Such men possess political authority, and have command of armies and police forces; but they do not possess tolerance or respect for alternative views. Unless restrained by democratic institutions and the rule of law – exactly what tyrants brush aside in irritation at the obstacles they present; for as Lucan warned, 'if a strong man does not get what he thinks is his due, he will take all he can' – they will have no reason to stop short of threatening, bullying, and finally 'disappearing' their enemies.

There are other kinds of power, no less harmful if in different ways. Consider media tycoons and their influence on the future of whole countries. They illustrate that the problem is not so much the mere existence of power, but its presence in ungoverned hands. 'The first principle of a civilised state,' said Walter Lippman, 'is that power is legitimate only when it is under contract.' The application of this principle is obvious as regards a government's power to enforce the laws it passes, and to keep order in its jurisdiction. Democracy is a contract by which the exercise of such power is kept responsible. But there are less obvious contracts constraining other kinds of power. The power to state an opinion publicly, for example, is subject to the unwritten contract of debate; the opinion can be disagreed with, its supporting arguments challenged, the facts on which it is based checked. This contract has been hard won in the course of modern history, because it is not long since it was fatally dangerous to disagree with the opinions of those in power, whether they were Popes in the Vatican or Party Secretaries in the Kremlin. In some places, the danger has not yet passed.

Power's tendency to corrupt is a function of the work it does in liberating man's worse characteristics. A man feels his power over another more acutely when he breaks the other's spirit than when he wins his respect. To have power over others is to be in a position to deprive them of choices and options, to bend them to one's will, to make use of them. Almost any sensibility can quickly decay into finding this pleasurable as well as convenient. How many SS men denied themselves the pleasure of absolute control over others when it was offered? Perhaps history never got the chance to record the heroism which such denial would truly represent. Unquestionably, to use real power gently, and for the good of others, is one of the most heroic of virtues; which is why examples of it are so rare.

Protest

Sometimes a scream is better than a thesis.

EMERSON

History is written by victors, and victors tend to be those who are, or shortly after their victory become, rich and powerful; and therefore we hear little, or anyway too little, about the history of those who have reason to protest at their subjugation by the rich and powerful. An alternative history of the world, if it were true and fair, would tell of the long, painful struggle of the majority to escape the heel of the minority, under which – now as throughout recorded time – the majority mainly languishes, if not indeed suffers. Rebellions, uprisings, hunger marches, Levellers, Luddites, Chartists, pacifists, resistance fighters, student activists, all belong to a tradition stretching back into earliest recorded times, representing the repeated, sporadic, too often futile endeavour of the oppressed to free themselves and get their due.

Serious protesters against 'global capitalism' belong to this tradition. They are concerned about the power of great business enterprises, many of them wealthier than many states, whose straddling of the globe makes them unaccountable to, and uncontrollable by, any single government. Critics dislike the way global corporations exploit labour in Third-World countries, moving from one to the next as workforces become skilled and start to demand better wages and conditions. The corporations often leave dirty footprints on the natural environment, and by their unremitting enslavement to present profit cannot be relied upon to think of the future good of the world, any more than they can be relied upon to care for the current good of their employees, whom they often treat as if they are as expendable as nature itself.

Many of market capitalism's critics wish not to erase but to improve it, by constraining the drive for profit in the interests of people and nature. Even in cut-throat America there are laws preventing monopolies and promoting workplace safety, thus admitting that unregulated capitalism is a menace. The serious protester's point is that global capitalism is too like unregulated capitalism – and therefore a menace likewise.

'Serious' implies its opposite. There are plenty of freeloaders in anti-globalisation protests. These are people who like to smash windows and dislodge policemen's helmets for the mere sake of the pleasure it affords. If they are motivated by anger, it is not at the plight of their less fortunate fellows, but because they resent the labour and deferral of present gratifications required to gain access to the rewards offered by capitalism. Familiarly, every serious demonstration about social and political matters is invariably joined, and often hijacked, by vandals and extremists, who thereby divert attention from the important questions at issue in the protest, and fill the next day's newspapers with endless reports and debates about violence, police tactics, injuries and arrests – thus robbing the protest of its point. One wonders if they are in the pay of those against whom the protest is directed; for these latter are the only ones who benefit from what they do.

Thoughtful challenges to the bad side of global capitalism focus upon injustice, which raises both moral and practical questions. On the best view, justice is fairness. If a pensioner needs 1500 calories a day and an athlete in training needs 4000, but you oblige them both to consume exactly 2000, you treat them equally – but unfairly. Thus justice is not equality but equity; as Aristotle says, 'Injustice arises when equals are treated unequally, and unequals are treated equally.'

The gross disparities between rich and poor, and the inequitable treatment received by Third-World workers – both hallmarks of global capitalism – are unjustifiable in themselves, and ultimately threaten capitalism itself. The practical point is obvious: instead of undertaking self-defeating scorched-earth activities, capitalism would be wise to encourage the flourishing of individuals and countries to provide itself rich markets in which to sell its goods and make profits. The moral point is equally obvious: there is no defensible reason for treating people differently only because some are not as effective as others at getting their demands met – which is the invariable fate of the poor and weak. It is on their behalf that protest is most justified because most needed.

Justice

All virtue is summed up in dealing justly.

ARISTOTLE

Institutions of law are essential to civilised society, yet they enshrine injustice. This paradox arises because systems of law are inherently conservative – sometimes for good reasons, sometimes for bad ones.

Good systems of justice embody the idea of 'due process'. This complex and ancient principle is based on the idea of an individual's right to a fair and public trial properly conducted, the right to be heard at his trial, and the right to an impartial jury. Moreover, it requires that all laws must be so framed that a reasonable person can understand them.

What is admirable about such systems of justice – which exist everywhere in the developed world; a non-accidental fact – is that they afford a means of peaceful resolution of the conflicts which arise between individuals, between interest groups, and between society and its members. Problems are considered, arguments on all sides are heard and weighed – and because they mostly involve pressing matters of practice, decisions are reached according to the law's best lights. In ideal circumstances, courts of law offer a forum where experienced and impartial minds can consider the merits of cases and offer practicable ways of resolving them. However imperfect such a system might in practice be, it is far preferable to arbitrary tyranny, to corruption, to gun-law, and to chance.

One of the chief benefits of due process is that it safeguards individuals against arbitrary arrest and interference by governments or their servants. It thus interposes an impartial, considered process between citizens and the sources of power in society. But the tardily formal application of general laws which are 'never quite appropriate for everyone', as Livy long ago remarked, together with the blindness of laws to unusual or special cases, and the painful slowness with which courts and legislatures change laws that have become worse than irrelevant – witness, for example, the long struggle to legalise homosexuality and abortion, and to roll back censorship – result in many injustices.

'Laws and institutions must go hand in hand with the progress of the human mind,' said Thomas Jefferson, one of the framers of the American Constitution; yet even in America legal conservatism retards progress, not least because the provisions of the Constitution itself, which are of unequal merit, all have equal sanctity – so that, for example, the now-absurd 'right to bear arms' is as fiercely defended as the right to free speech. The progress of the human mind is more rapid than the evolution of legal institutions; and uncertainty or lack of confidence, masquerading as caution, on the part of governments and judges alike, is an anchor holding back the advances needed by society when opinion and circumstances call for change.

Justice delayed is injustice. Robert Kennedy once added that justice delayed is also democracy denied. Of course, one cannot expect laws to change at the whim of mass sentiment; such was the way in primitive conditions of society, which, if they were now to return, would inevitably result in bodies hanging from lamp-posts, on mere suspicion of hated crimes like paedophilia. But a society's laws have to be responsive to new circumstances, and one way they can be so is for those who operate them to be imaginative, sympathetic, and themselves representative of the society they serve. In the nature of things, members of judiciaries are seldom all three at once; and they are too frequently none of the three.

One thought prompted by the foregoing is that justice often seems to be a penalty exacted from the present by the past. Anatole France caustically observed that 'justice is the sanction of established injustice', thinking of the way that original inequities in the distribution of wealth, power and privilege in society come in time to be sanctified by history and protected by law – and of the way old laws keep old prohibitions alive beyond their day. It is this resistance to change that threatens to make justice unjust, and requires at the very least that the servants of justice should try, if they can, to turn towards the future when they judge.

Liberty

He sets his guards about us, as in Freedom's name.

KIPLING

As the angry gloom of Fascism and impending war massed over Europe in the 1930s, an international congress of writers assembled in Paris to discuss the threat to freedom posed by the increasingly harsh and illiberal laws being passed not only in Hitler's Germany and Mussolini's Italy, but in countries traditionally jealous of liberty, such as England and France.

One speaker at the congress was E. M. Forster. Then and in the war years that followed Forster was a quiet but doughty spokesman for civil liberties, a fact forgotten now that it is fashionable to slight his fiction and asperse the nature of his sympathies for Britain's colonised. After acknowledging the proper limitations on British pride in its long-cherished liberties – these being the racism of its colonial policies and its oppressive domestic class structure – he said that he was not afraid of Oswald Mosley's black-shirted Fascists but instead of what he called 'fabio-Fascism', by which he meant 'the dictator-spirit working quietly away behind the façade of constitutional forms, passing a little law (like the Sedition Act) here, endorsing a departmental tyranny there, emphasising the national need for secrecy elsewhere' – and then he quoted Kipling describing how a tyrant works:

He shall mark our goings, question whence we came,
Set his guards about us, as in Freedom's name.
He shall peep and mutter, and night shall bring
Watchers 'neath our window, lest we mock the King.

What Forster understood was that it is precisely in times of
emergency that a people has to be most vigorous in defending
its civil liberties, for that is when governments take the opportunity to limit them, preaching necessity. In 1911, as the result
of the now forgotten Agadir Incident in Morocco which resulted
in the transfer of the Congo from France to Germany, thus
putatively compromising Britain's imperial interests in Africa,
a law was passed in a single day's sitting in Parliament – the
reviled, harmful, wretched Official Secrets Act of unlamented
memory, which, so hastily passed, stubbornly resisted repeal
thereafter, and caused decades of difficulty.

It is a strange sad fact that the exact number of dead in the mass
murders of 11 September 2001 in New York and Washington
might never be known. Some among the victims were illegal
immigrants, working as cleaners and labourers. The nature of
the catastrophe made it difficult to identify, even to find, the
dead. One bitter estimate says that perhaps more than a thousand children lost a parent in the atrocities.

But the larger count of 11 September's victims is even harder
to compute. Additional deaths occurred in Afghanistan and
elsewhere in military actions taken to revenge them. Most
cruelly, an estimate made by the World Bank projected 30,000
extra infant deaths world-wide for the ensuing twelve months,
on the grounds that the terrorism-steepened world recession
would push 10 million people below the poverty income of $1
a day – and infant death is poverty's bedfellow.

Such are the fruits of xenophobia, dogma and callousness,
which lead humans to inflict wretchedness on other humans in

the name of one or another abstraction. But there are other victims besides, not least among them civil liberties. Politicians react to terrorism by limiting liberties, the West's most cherished possession, in hopes of facilitating the capture of the minuscule percentage of people who are zealots intent on perpetrating atrocities.

Even if restrictions upon whole populations could deter terrorists – which is highly unlikely – the mere fact of going so far is tantamount to yielding too much to the terrorists who assault liberal societies and seek to reinstate ancient oppressions in them. The keystones of liberal society are individual autonomy and mutual tolerance, and even though both are indeed properly subject to limits, the limits should be such as to protect what is most valuable in them, not to compromise them. Zealots, most especially religious zealots, hate the liberality of liberal society; their terrorism aims to destroy it. To start putting handcuffs on ourselves is to achieve their goals for them.

Tolerance is not only a key feature of liberalism, but – familiarly – its paradox too. Liberalism's tolerance leaves the democracy of ideas to decide which among opposing viewpoints will prevail. The risk is the death of liberty itself, because those who live by hard and uncompromising views in political, moral and religious respects always, if given half a chance, silence liberals because liberalism, by its nature, threatens the hegemony they seek to impose.

So it is endlessly worth iterating that the answer to the question, 'Should the tolerant tolerate the intolerant?' must be a mighty and resounding 'No.' Liberal society can oppose intolerance by living up to the principle that anyone can put a point of view, but no one can be forced to accept it. The only coercion should be that of argument, the only obligation that of honest reasoning. But when anyone tries to bully others into his own point of view, he should be brought up short. It is the technique of the baboon to try to get its way by violence. The way of civilised human beings is to live and let live. Alas, violence sometimes invites nothing other than more of itself as the only possible defence.

Among the points worth remembering about liberty, these three are chief: that, as Judge Hand remarked, liberty is about allowing alternatives and promoting open-mindedness; that, in Thomas Paine's words, 'he that would make his own liberty secure must guard even his enemy from oppression'; and that liberty does not come free, but at the price of vigilance – and of sacrifice when the need arises.

Pluralism

Antipathies between different ethnicities or cultures, especially when they flare into violence, are dismaying because they threaten to dash the brave hope that multiculturalism is possible – the hope, in other words, that communities of varied backgrounds and outlooks, histories and values, can coexist by mutual tolerance and respect.

When such outbursts happen – they seem mainly to come in summer, in hot weather, starting in the long light evenings when young men are on the streets, ready to give and take offence – the reaction is either to preach integration, by whose means differences are effaced; or segregation, which erects walls between groups. Integrationists speak of a 'melting pot', which the United States once hoped to be. Optimists thought that the crucible of that country's young aspirations would forge the clamorous disparities of the old world into a new entity. Integration has not happened there, nor has the different process of assimilation, which typically affects small groups submerged in larger ones. Internecine friction remains commonplace in America, always in the poorer quarters of its big cities.

Segregationists claim that their view is the only realistic one, because it accepts as a fact the proposition that human differences are irreducible. Their approach ranges from the apartheid of South Africa and the southern states of the USA, to calls for repatriation of immigrants and opposition to further immigration. In places like Northern Ireland their pessimism results in the literal building of brick walls between communities.

But neither of these responses is the right one. Multiculturalism can work; and the proof is, that it does work. It works most of the time in most places in the world. Sporadic outbursts of conflict, or sore spots where tensions simmer, are inevitable; but for the many highly idiosyncratic groups of people – ethnically, culturally, and religiously diverse, with strong senses of identity, and strong nostalgic attachments to former lands and other ways – which make up the big Western nations, life is mostly peaceful.

Western societies by their nature encompass a plurality of values. Most liberals have faith in the idea that tolerance and debate can resolve conflicts of values and bring about harmony. This is a legacy of Enlightenment attitudes, premised on the belief that because human beings everywhere have much in common, agreement about how to live in peace is possible. This view provides the basis for the concept of universal human rights, and the practice of negotiating international agreements affecting many aspects of the relations between people and states in an increasingly interconnected world. And this is consistent with the continued existence of different cultures and traditions; indeed, it premises the idea that differences should be encouraged, as a good thing in their own right.

But this faith is opposed by those who argue that the difference in values of different groups makes serious conflicts inevitable, and that because there are no neutral ways to resolve them, the world is doomed to suffer and perhaps be destroyed by them – unless one group conquers the rest.

It has become fashionable to call this relativistic pessimism

'Post-modern', but it already existed in the eighteenth century, and was strengthened by Romanticism, which sees particularity and self-expression as fundamentals, not just for individuals but for cultural identities. In the nineteenth century some aspects of Romanticism supported nationalism, and nationalism supported racism, thereby making compost for the horrors of the twentieth century.

Many liberal supporters of multiculturalism say that even if there were a germ of truth in relativism – which would mean accepting that societies which attempt to give peaceful house-room to different traditions are condemned to irreducible internal conflicts – it remains worthwhile to insist on efforts at mutual toleration; for, what is the option? Since neither segregationist nor integrationist alternatives work, tolerance and reason are the only way to help maintain that equilibrium which is the fundamental requirement of a decent society.

Anger and War

Anger

Anger is the chief emotion driving the deadly reciprocity of reprisal and revenge which has engulfed the recent history of the Middle East. The other dominating emotions of that tragedy – grief and terror – would bring the violence to an end without it. But anger, bitter and implacable when the only response it gets is anger returned, feeds on its reflection until it becomes insanity.

'Angry men are blind and foolish,' Aretino wrote, 'for reason at such times takes flight, and in her absence anger plunders all the riches of the intellect.' When given expression it plunders all the goods and fruits of peace too, and is indifferent to the suffering of bystanding innocents. The angry man's desire is to vent his heat, to appease himself by doing harm, not pausing to consider whether the greatest harm will eventually accrue to himself rather than his opponent. And when anger drives, such is the usual outcome.

The ancients debated anger extensively. For the Stoics it was an emotion of weakness, to be quelled as part of building self-mastery and detachment. In a sequence of three carefully considered *Moral Essays* Seneca analysed anger, 'the most hideous and frenzied of all the emotions', and urged the classic Stoic remedy: the restraint of the heroic mind. Failing that, he said, 'there are two rules: avoid anger if you can, and if you cannot, in your anger do no wrong.'

Others saw anger as an emotion capable of great power and good effect if wisely directed. 'It is easy to fly into a passion,' Aristotle remarked, 'anyone can do that; but to be angry with the right person, to the right extent, at the right time, in the right way, with the right aim; that is not easy.' His view is that knowing how to be appropriately angry is an essential part of the moral life – providing that it does not overthrow reason and become merely destructive in consequence. 'A man that does not know how to be angry does not know how to be good,' is Beecher's modern Aristotelian gloss.

But in vitriolic conflicts there is neither appropriateness nor proportion, so the arguments of history and justice become lost in vengeance. Rabidly angry men want only to fight; they want to inflict anguish on their enemies, and then obliterate them. It is hard to imagine, even if great-souled people stood up on both sides and agreed peace and a *modus vivendi*, how such hurt could be assuaged. 'No man is angry that feels not himself hurt,' Bacon said, and the trouble is that adversaries have invariably become such because of hurts, real or perceived.

Each side in an angry conflict of course wishes to win. But what would winning involve? Hard men think it involves breaking and trampling the enemy, killing him or driving him away either geographically or into a psychological diaspora of submission. But it takes scarcely any thought, so long as it is calm thought, to see that victory is never achieved until anger subsides and both sides gain at least some of their aims.

The first great poem in world literature is about anger and its terrible consequences. Homer's *Iliad* begins: 'The wrath of Achilles is my theme, the fatal wrath which, fulfilling Zeus's will, brought the Achaeans so much suffering, and sent so many noble souls to Hades, leaving their bodies as carrion for vultures and dogs.' Homer tells a vast morality tale, stemming from the quarrel between Achilles and Agamemnon over a division of spoils, involving a girl called Briseis who was confiscated by Agamemnon from Achilles, to the latter's implacable rage. Their feud weakens the Greek army, which suffers repeated defeats; Achilles' own beloved friend Patroclus is killed by Hector, whom Achilles kills in revenge, and then cruelly drags round Troy's walls behind his chariot.

For Homer's Greeks, therefore, as for those after them everywhere who are urgent for revenge, the words of Proverbs are apt: 'He that is slow to anger is better than the mighty; and he that ruleth his spirit than he that taketh a city.'

Conflict

Wars of opinion, as they have been the most destructive, are the most disgraceful of conflicts, being appeals from right to might and from argument to artillery.

CHARLES CALEB COLTON

It would be encouraging to think that when conflicts cannot end in outright victory for one side, they tend to end in weariness and a growing sickness at the waste they cause. If this were so, conflict would be self-limiting, dying down as a fire does when it has consumed its fuel. But human conflicts seem to defy this hope. They pause, and for a time there is a simulacrum of peace; but grudges are passed like heritable diseases from one generation to the next, and there is always dry tinder in the human stock ready to catch alight when friction is renewed.

History is rich in examples of this dismal lesson. The Balkans, the Middle East, Indonesia, Kashmir and Central Africa provide contemporary instances, but it would be a mistake to think conflict naturally belongs to dispensations outside the charmed circle of Western democracies. Ireland, two world wars and the United States' catastrophe in Vietnam prove otherwise; the selfsame infection took hold in these cases, involving what some of the participants liked to think were the richest, most developed and civilised polities in the world.

What are the sources of these conflicts? It is natural to think they share deep common roots in the fact that resources are few, people many. Competition over resources can easily turn into conflict. Societies evolve means for adjudicating disputes among the individuals and interest groups constituting them, chiefly by institutional means like government and law; but sometimes the conflict is too great even for that safeguard. The same applies in the international sphere, where on a larger scale the same cost is exacted by failure – namely, bloodshed and destruction.

But there is one thing wrong with this picture. It mislocates the roots of conflict in competition over resources, the model being imagined tribes of early man quarrelling over access to water-holes or pastures. No doubt such things happened. But the real reason for the bitterness and persistence of human conflicts has little to do with resources and everything to do with ideology, opinions, beliefs and traditions.

The recent discovery that humans have only twice as many genes as fruitflies has tipped the balance in the nature-nurture debate back to nurture. On this evidence it is our culture, history and belief-systems which make us what we are. We look at the rest of nature and see carnivores killing to eat, but we do not see zebras forming armies to wage war on gnus. It is only humans, with their congenital vice of inventing differences of politics and faith, who murder one another because they disagree. And what makes the tragedy more poignant is that the less secure their grounds for belief, the more anxious and violent their adherence to it – and the greater their readiness to kill and die in its defence.

Guns

He has made his weapons his gods. When his weapons win, he is defeated himself.

RABINDRANATH TAGORE

It is a frightening fact that there are hundreds of millions of cheap guns available in the world. The United Nations makes efforts to find ways of containing the international trade in arms, but it is opposed either overtly or covertly by the nations which manufacture and export them.

It is worth keeping some simple facts in mind. A gun is a device expressly designed for killing things. It is a tube fitted with mechanisms engineered to project hard objects as forcefully as possible, the aim being to pierce and fatally damage the bodies of living creatures. As technology has improved – note the word 'improved' – so the efficiency of guns, their power, range, accuracy, and general murderous effect, has increased. The ease with which birds and beasts, men, women and children, can now be shot into sudden oblivion is breathtaking. If a murderer had nothing but his hands, he could kill only a few on a single outing, if lucky. But a victim might fight back, and win. What a limitation, a frustration, for the poor murderer. But with a Kalashnikov – joy! – all such frustration vanishes. In a few seconds dozens of human beings can be left twitching and bleeding on the ground, their possibilities, hopes, loves and endeavours abruptly and arbitrarily obliterated, their families drowned in shock and grief. How satisfying for the murderous of mind; how fulfilling; and all thanks to those who make and sell guns.

Obviously therefore a gun is a glorious thing, a beautiful testament to the wisdom, refinement and superiority of the human imagination. Arms manufacturers must be proud of the benefit they confer on humanity, in providing it with these ready means to kill and maim, to wage war, to assassinate, to settle tribal feuds and fine points of theology or ideology – and when not being aimed at people, their source of profit can be used instead to slaughter pheasants on British moors, tusk-bearing elephants on the African savannah, tigers in Bengal, and bears in China where bear-paw soup is such a delicacy. How barbarous it is, the gun-makers must think, that seal-cubs are beaten to death when a gun would do the work so much less wearingly.

It must be nice, therefore, to be an arms manufacturer. Investing in arms companies is like buying gilts, so secure are their sales, so bottomless the demand they satisfy; for conflict is in endless supply, given that men will always find reasons to hate and kill each other. Guns thus breed the need for more guns. No government on earth imposes restrictions on the manufacture and sale of arms – or anyway, restrictions effective enough to stop guns reaching the buyers that want them: the terrorists, the leaders of boy-soldiers in the poorest and saddest places on earth, the crazed religious fanatics, the solitary fantasising stalkers, the neo-nazis and anarchists of the American Midwest. So to be an arms manufacturer is to be guaranteed a rich, happy and peaceful life, free from care. Arms manufacturers can eat well, take pleasant holidays, and sleep contentedly, knowing that the money they make from selling ever more guns keeps them well away from the harm those guns do.

But let us hope a small voice disturbs that sleep at times, saying that the existence of guns – of instruments designed, engineered, polished and oiled for the purpose of killing things, mainly people – is a scandal, an evil, a strange, profoundly disturbing comment on human nature. Adorno remarked that the illusion of human progress is exposed by the difference between the spear and the guided missile, showing that humans have grown cleverer but not wiser through history. It is a devastating reflection on our moral health that guns are not rarer than gold, and harder to find than peace in the present gun-infested misery of the world.

War

War is both the product of an earlier corruption and the producer of new corruptions.

LEWIS MUMFORD

War, always an evil, is sometimes the lesser of two evils. Even then it needs additional justification, from the degree of evil it opposes. The war against Nazism was a justified war, although not everything done in it by the opponents of Nazism was justified. This consideration prompts the inescapable question about the conduct of war: what should be its limits? Should ethics tie one's hands when faced with an implacable enemy, whose victory would be a disaster for the world? Churchill said, 'There is no middle course in wartime.' This hard truth forces one to recognise another: that every war, however justified, reduces the stock of human good, and diminishes civilisation – sometimes destroying in seconds what centuries built.

War prompted by religion, even indirectly, is never justified. Whatever the proximate excuse for such wars, the basis of each one is exactly the same, namely, suspicion and hostility engendered by differences of belief and associated culture. Christian armies mounted crusades against 'infidels' to capture the holy places of the Middle East, and against 'heretics' such as the Cathars to rebut their falsehoods by exterminating those who believed them. These are entirely matters of ideology. None of the major faiths is bloodless; history reeks with the gore of their wars and persecutions, all the more disgusting a spectacle for being, in essence, as simple as this: A kills B because B does not agree with A that there are fairies at the bottom of the garden.

People should be left to believe what they like, so long as they harm no one else. Apart from normal expectations of politeness, it is not however clear why people should require their personal beliefs to be treated with special sensitivity by others, to the point that if others fail to tip-toe respectfully around them they will start throwing bombs. From a secular point of view, religious beliefs are at best absurd and at worst dangerous, and the amount of free play they are given in the public domain is a menace. Believed-in fairies should be kept at home as an entirely private matter, and their votaries encouraged to cease taking themselves so seriously that, when irritated by those who differ, they resort to Kalashnikovs. Apart from anything else, such reactions speak little confidence in their own vio-lently-held certainties.

When differences of belief and religion-based culture are the ultimate source of conflict, the real war that needs to be fought is the war of ideas. A secularist might hope that liberal scientific education would at last free the human spirit from its thraldom to ancient superstitions and practices. Realism prompts the more modest hope that people can learn to accept that others differ, that belief is a private matter, and that no one has the right to impose beliefs on others or to punish their non-acceptance.

This aspiration has a practical dimension. In order to accom-modate a variety of religious and cultural differences in a single society, society itself needs to be wholly secular, most especially its educational institutions. 'Faith-based' schools entrench and perpetuate the differences which too often lead to conflict; by educating children from all backgrounds together there is a far greater chance of mutual understanding and personal friend-ships. Enthusiasts of all faiths oppose secular education because exposure to other traditions has the effect of loosening the grip of their own. That, from a secular standpoint, is of course the consummation devoutly to be wished.

The war of ideas today is what makes a difference to the occurrence or otherwise of shooting wars tomorrow. But the murderous grip of humanity's various immemorial belief-systems is unavoidably here now, sprouting its bitter fruit. It is as hard for the innocents of one side to defend against the frenzy of fanatics as for those of the other to protect themselves against technological might. But the survivors, if there are any, can try to defend the future by winning the longer and greater war against the intolerance, bigotry, zealotry and hatred which so brutally divides humankind against itself.

War's Causes

Blood is the god of war's rich livery.

MARLOWE

Discussions of the causes of war – not of this or that war, but of the phenomenon of war in general – sometimes conflate two different matters. One is an interesting set of speculations about the psychological place of war in human history. The other, drinking from the tainted well of Freudian theory, is a painfully improbable and confused account of the origins of that psychology in a suppositious prehistory of mankind – using, alas, the dodgy armchair logic typical of amateurs in the genre, inferring 'it is' from 'perhaps' and 'it's possible', these premises themselves inflated from the archaeological scraps of bone and shards of flint constituting the sum of current evidence in the field.

According to this latter line of thinking, our early ancestors – as small unmuscular primates lacking sharp teeth and claws – began by occupying a slot in the food chain as prey. Their later graduation to predator status did not eliminate the legacies of preyhood, namely, alarm in the face of threat, and a propensity to collective self-defence. These emotions, first learned from the experience of 'a primal battle that the entire human species might easily have lost', as one amateur put it, are carried into the predator phase. They prompt religious practices, chiefly blood sacrifice of people or animals. When the herds of large ungulates hunted by our ancestors diminished, they – at least, the males – began to hunt each other instead. Thus war.

Central to this view are the claims that hunting is 'violent', represents 'conflict' between humans and animals, and gives rise to blood-centred sacrificial religion; and further, that in the absence of opportunities to kill (other) animals, humans resort to killing one another as, in effect, a cure for boredom. The two first are conceptual mistakes, the third a feeble attempt to force a link between hunting and war, when there are much closer and more varied links between hunting and sports – such as running, throwing, and team games. (Among early humans, games would have been an effective and economical way of training for, and replacing, hunting; war suggests much more serious interests at stake. But this too is guesswork.)

Above all, the amateurs in this field are prone to fall for the modern gothic myth that blood is an especially lurid symbol of strife and danger. But until the recent past, blood was an ordinary enough concomitant of daily life, as when a chicken was carried from the coop for dinner, or the family pig was stuck, or a mare foaled in the paddock. People still make sausages out of blood in some quarters. Such were lately commonplaces of life; their absence today makes them significant enough to explain Quentin Tarantino. And as to religious sacrifices: they were ways of giving the gods a propitiatory or thanksgiving share, and were by no means restricted to blood and flesh; indeed they were more usually vegetable.

More interesting and useful material becomes available when we turn attention to the logistics of war, and particularly to the important point that large-scale organised war is the development that gave birth to one of the most evil monstrosities of modern times, viz. Nationalism. Both points are telling. Large armies and the logistics of their operation require bureaucracies to collect the taxes and sustain the paperwork necessary. This is part, at least – but a significant part – of the reason why the modern nation state came into existence. It is a curiosity that people can die for the Fatherland, feel their hearts swell at the marching rhythm of the Marseillaise, and worship the Stars and Stripes, when these all represent ill-defined abstractions of a very artificial kind, masking the logic of bureaucracy and taxation. But it is a tragic curiosity.

Equally important is the question of what war is not. War is not simply a matter of aggressive emotions – although these, when mobilised among a country's population by its politicians, can provide a powerful impetus to the starting of wars. In the past, when soldiers fought hand to hand, they needed alcohol and other drugs to prompt them into an appropriately murderous mood. But in modern armies, cool calculation and methodical organisation are vital. War is not a pub brawl, and therefore does not derive from the excess testosterone of individual young males; it merely annexes that hormone for its own purposes. What those purposes are is legion: there are very many specific reasons why particular wars start, and if we concern ourselves only with war in the abstract in order to discover why humans organise themselves to wage it, we misdirect ourselves. The many reasons why wars occur together explain the reason why war occurs: there is no single psychological feature of mankind – no extra, occult, prehistoric, instinctive thing – which alone explains the frequent and repeated madness of war, and the fact that most societies devote such vast proportions of their resources to preparing for it. Plenty of quasi-Freudians claim to know what it is in the psyche of mankind that is to blame; but one would do better to ask economists and historians of diplomacy for the explanation.

Western Victories

The quickest way to end a war is by losing it.

ORWELL

On 11 October 732 Islamic warriors reached the northernmost point of their invasion of Europe – the road between Poitiers and Tours, less than 200 miles south of Paris. As Gibbon observed in pondering that fateful day, if they had been allowed to travel as far again as the distance they had already covered from Gibraltar, the Muslim armies would have reached Scotland or Poland; in which case, he mused, the Koran 'would now be taught in the schools of Oxford, whose pupils might demonstrate to a circumcised people the sanctity and truth of the revelation of Mahomet.'

But the Muslims were denied by Charles Martel – 'Martel' being a sobriquet meaning 'the Hammer' – father of Pippin and grandfather of Charlemagne, who turned the course of history by defeating the invaders at Poitiers. It had been a mere century since the death of the Prophet, and Islam had swept like a firestorm across the Middle East and Central Asia to the banks of the Indus, and along North Africa and over the Iberian peninsular, making converts at the edge of the sword. Its technique of conquest was lightning cavalry strikes and the spread of terror. But Charles Martel's heavily armed Frankish infantry, disciplined and determined, stood like a 'wall of ice' against which the Muslim cavalry charges dashed and broke. From that day began the long-drawn *reconquista* which eventually pushed Islam out of Western Europe.

According to some historians, the battle of Poitiers is one of a number of salient examples of how cultural factors explain the military supremacy of the West – and not just from the sixteenth century AD onwards when Western industrial and technological superiority becomes obvious, but from the very beginning of distinctively Western culture, viz. at the time of the Persian War in the fifth century BC. These cultural factors explain why the history of warfare is so often the history of Western victories.

The reason was identified long ago by the Spartan general Brasidas, as reported by Thucydides. Brasidas told his troops before their encounter with the barbarians of Illyria that they had nothing to fear from them; they are a mob, he said, unlike we disciplined Spartans, for they are the product of a culture 'in which the many do not rule the few, but rather the few the many'. This implies that the secret of Western success lies in the fact that its soldiers are free men with a stake beyond mere booty in the outcome of the wars they fight.

According to the historian Victor Hanson, this ethos was forged in the classical civilisations of Greece and Rome and bequeathed by them to all Europe. Its main components are those that were or have since given rise to the kind of liberal democracies now typical of the West, characterised by economic success and free debate. In historical terms, European armies were always principally composed of heavily-armed infantrymen who in civilian life were freemen with their own farms, not slaves or serfs. The battles of Salamis, Gaugamela, Cannae, Poitiers, Lepanto and others offer evidence, in the view of historians who share Hanson's opinion, for the thesis that the open culture of free men lies at the root of the West's military supremacy.

This view is supported by recent examples of Western military success. In the Gulf War a US-led military coalition operating far from home defeated a 1.2-million-strong army, equipped with 6000 tanks, on its own terrain, in just four days, for the loss of 150 personnel. None of Iraq's troops had voted to invade Kuwait, Hanson observes; Saddam's plans were not subject to journalistic probing or parliamentary audit; all his military hardware was imported. The Iraqi army 'was nearly annihilated not far from the battlefields of Cunaxa and Gaugamela, where Xenophon's Ten Thousand and Alexander the Great had likewise routed indigenous Asian imperial armies so long ago.' Even more recently, the long reach of superior military technology and highly trained volunteer service personnel repeated the success in Afghanistan, where the enemy, although smaller and weaker by far than the Iraqi army, had considerable guerrilla advantages.

This confident, not to say triumphalist, thesis sounds brash in the difficult circumstances in which the West and its values find themselves after September 2001. But there may well be something right about it. Part of the story is doubtless this: that the West has won so often because victories make further victories possible, consolidated over time because Europe and its extension to North America has been the home of the scientific and industrial revolutions. It is certainly right to say that until now the West's biggest enemy has been itself, as the terrible wars of the twentieth century attest. Its main hope must be that this is no longer true.

Triumph

It is almost as easy to be enervated by triumph as by defeat.
MAX LERNER

Naturally enough, a victory is more triumphant when unexpectedly won against the odds than when confidently anticipated. By the same token, a victory which is less in scale than predicted can feel like a defeat, especially when the opponent claims a moral success after all. The latter kind excepted, victories are nevertheless usually experienced as triumphs for the simple but irreducible reason that winning feels good, thereby buoying the victor, refreshing his endeavours, and serving as a justification for everything that led up to them. Many victories have been granted by losers rather than gained by winners, but even here the latter's jubilation is scarcely alloyed by the manner of the event; for at the moment it happens, winning is always enough.

But only at the moment it happens, for victory never comes free. Speaking as one who well knew both sides of the equation, Churchill said, 'The problems of victory are more agreeable than those of defeat, but no less difficult.' His remark is a reminder that victory, especially in politics, is only ever the beginning of a hard road – namely, the labour of getting an uncertain chance to win again.

Originally a triumph was an ancient Roman celebratory procession awarded to generals who had won important battles. It was a ritual governed by strict rules; no general's remit ran in Rome itself, so when he returned from his campaign the successful general had to wait outside the city walls while the Senate suspended the law – for one day only – to allow him to enter with his army. In order to merit a triumph a general had to have won a decisive victory in which his troops killed more than 5000 of the enemy while sustaining relatively light casualties themselves. Not every general could expect a triumph even when these conditions were met; he had also to hold the rank of magistrate at least. Scipio Africanus, after his amazing feats of generalship in Spain, was granted only an *ovatio* because he was insufficiently senior.

A triumphant general was given a warm welcome. Standing in a four-horse chariot, accompanied by toga-clad senators, followed by his booty and captives, and surrounded by his troops shouting '*Io triumphe!*' and singing coarse songs, he made his way through huge applauding crowds along the Via Sacra to the temple of Jupiter Capitolinus, there to sacrifice an assortment of animals to the king of the gods, and to offer up the bay-leaf wreathe which the Senate had placed on his brow as the sign of his success.

The most important person in the triumphal procession was not, however, the general himself, but the slave who stood with him in his chariot. It was this slave's duty, as the procession wound its way through the cheers, to whisper warnings into the general's ear, to help him guard against the consequences of pride, arrogance, overweening self-belief, loss of perspective, and forgetfulness of home truths. 'You are mortal,' whispered the slave. 'Remember, the gods are jealous. Disaster might follow triumph, and when it does it can be all the more devastating therefore. Success breeds many enemies. Unless you are magnanimous in victory, you might one day taste the bitterness of defeat. Homer said: "It is man's lot to fight, but fate alone grants success." Men are never truly conquered by arms, but by love and reason; so far, you have only conquered by arms.' And so on.

Hubris, as the slave's whispers show, is one risk of triumph. Another is its tendency to invite repose, relaxation, a dropped guard. In either case it invites future defeat. The only way to make good use of triumph is to think of it as belonging to something else – the causes you care for, the people you represent, the future good of things, the possibility for progressive, imaginative, generous alternatives to whatever is wrong or lacking in the world. When a general saw his triumph as belonging to Rome rather than himself, he had no need of the slave's admonitions. Every victor would do well not to need the slave likewise.

Safety

According to the *Panchatantra* – an ancient collection of Sanskrit tales written to teach good conduct to princes – 'safety is the greatest gift in the world, better than the gift of a cow, of land, or of food'. Most would agree, thinking how dangerous a place the world seems, beset as it is by acts of terrorism, by natural and man-made disasters, and by the fatalities of war. For people in quarters of the globe usually as peaceful as they are rich, it is something new to have perils and threats pressing so close, distorting the contours of a psychological landscape that once seemed pleasantly familiar and comfortably safe.

In poorer parts of the world, where the hostile interests of man and the brutal indifference of nature frequently prey on human security, safety has been a dream only ever realised, if at all, in small and temporary ways: as when there has been rain for the crops, or warlords have called an armistice. Now everywhere seems like that, with peace no more than a stressful intermission of strife, and safety just a brief interlude among dangers.

The dominant school of thought among educated people in classical antiquity was Stoicism, which taught how to achieve *ataraxia* – peace of mind – in an uncertain and fraught world.

You have little control over what happens in the world around you, the Stoics said, so you must accept with grace and resignation what it does to you. But you can govern your own emotions, and if you master them you will free yourself from anxiety. One aspect of the Stoic outlook is given succinct modern expression by Joseph Krutch: 'Security depends not upon how much you have, as upon how much you can do without.'

It is rational to take thought for one's safety. 'It is folly to bolt a door with a boiled carrot,' says the English proverb. But too much concern with safety – too little preparedness to accept that the very act of living is risky – is counter-productive in too many ways. To make everything yield to considerations of safety is to invite a different risk: that of living without opportunity, progress, or growth. 'The most beaten paths are certainly the surest,' said Andre Gide, 'but do not hope to start much game on them.'

This applies to personal life, not to such matters as airline safety, where no risks are acceptable. In personal life risks are the motors of advance, especially in emotional and intellectual respects. To love is to risk, to try new ideas and methods is to risk, to be open to new friendships, new experiences, new challenges and changes, all involve risks. The costs are occasional failure and the likelihood of suffering; but the prizes are great.

Governments which, in response to threats against the liberties and securities of the state, diminish the state's liberties in the hope of increasing its securities, thereby give a partial victory to the threateners. Benjamin Franklin acidly remarked that 'they that can give up essential liberty to obtain a little temporary safety deserve neither liberty nor safety'. It is better to live a trifle more dangerously to live freely, than to live safely in a locked room made of fears and restrictions – not least when the liberties in question have been hard won over long stretches of history, and are precious.

If small countries and quiet nations – places and peoples on the sidelines – are safe from terrorism, it is because they owe their immunity to their marginality. The same applies to individuals. In his Fable of the Great and Little Fishes Aesop has the latter say, 'Our insignificance is often the cause of our safety.' Some therefore embrace insignificance. But safety is almost its only merit. Although being out in front assuredly invites perils as well as rewards, there is the added consolation identified by Victor Hugo: 'Great perils have this beauty, that they bring to light the fraternity of strangers.'

War Crimes

Great crimes never come singly; they are linked to sins that went before.

RACINE

Scarcely any major country in the world has been innocent of war crimes and crimes against humanity in the last hundred years – and that includes Britain, the United States, France, even Switzerland, let alone the egregious examples of Nazi Germany and Soviet Russia. Nevertheless, as the twenty-first century got under way, the international community seemed increasingly determined not to let tyrants and butchers go unpunished for repeats of such crimes. It would be wrong not to bring the weight of human rights law against violators on the principle that only the sinless can accuse. If that were the rule, there would be no such thing as justice anywhere.

When the Nuremberg tribunal was instituted after the Second World War to prosecute captured Nazi leaders, chief among them Hermann Goring, Albert Speer and Admiral Donitz (the other principals were dead, mainly by suicide), there was no body of law to serve as the basis for the trial. A charter was drafted to give the tribunal a remit, and it effectively invented the concepts of 'war crimes' and 'crimes against humanity' for the purpose. Even at the time jurisprudents worried that the accused were being tried according to laws invented after their crimes were committed – a breach of fundamental notions of legality – and that all the prosecuting nations were in various ways and to various degrees themselves guilty of some of the same crimes.

But the scale of Nazi atrocities, and the need for a large gesture of international condemnation of military aggression and especially the Holocaust, made Nuremberg a necessity. It showed that there is a difference between law and justice – that justice can be done even in the absence of law – and the proceeding earned retrospective endorsement from the fact that it created the precedent for what has since been codified in the United Nations' two great Covenants on human rights, and the various national human rights instruments adopted by many countries since.

The growth of human rights awareness and concern in the last half-century is one of the most positive and optimistic legal-political developments ever to happen in world history – and that is not hyperbole, just plain fact. But its chief weakness has been lack of enforcement. Until very recently there was no means of bringing violators to justice, and no court to do it in. But that is changing. Greater use of *ad hoc* tribunals remedies the latter problem, and the preparedness of United Nations troops to seek war criminals helps to address the former problem.

These are healthy signs, and best of them is the United Nations' decision to institute an International Criminal Court. Not long beforehand President Clinton, standing in Rwanda's killing fields, had said, 'We must make it clear to all those who would commit such acts in the future that they too must answer for them, and they will.' If his words were an augury, the momentum of history is running in the right direction at last.

Vengeance

*It is difficult to fight against anger, for a man will buy
vengeance with his soul.*

HERACLITUS

Terrorist atrocities, which provoke acts of vengeance, are
themselves likely to be claimed as acts of vengeance by their
perpetrators, making a pattern now too familiar: hatred-fuelled
fanaticism, induced by resentment and an unappeasable sense
of injury, prompting acts of murderous violence on civilians
and bystanders, thereby inciting as response yet more of what
inflamed it in the first place. Terrorism is the aggression of the
weak, impotence made terribly potent by what, in its bald
simplicity, malignant rage is prepared to do: to kill anyone
indiscriminately so long as they are of the enemy's people, even
if in the process one dies oneself.

Some will say that the only way to deal with such fanatics it
to exterminate them, like disease-bearing vermin fit only for
poisoning or gassing. Literal-minded folk will point to the
ancient doctrine of an eye for an eye – the text in question
continues, 'burning for burning, wound for wound'.

What terrorists want is to puncture the pride, weaken the
power, insult the self image, and profoundly grieve the people
of their enemy. They regard themselves as having not just an
excuse but a duty to do so, in light of what they take to be
offences for which their own aggressions are themselves acts of

revenge. It is a bitter and relentless spiral. Part of the right response is to offer friendship to the communities from within which terrorism comes – to help them develop, healing the wounds of resentment, and bringing them fully into the international fraternity of co-operation. Doing so will not end terrorism, because it only takes a few lunatics to hold the world to ransom; but it will limit it, and open the possibility, at least, of a time when it again becomes rare.

Another response – a familiar but unquestionably right point, this – is to refuse to yield too much normal life to fear of terrorist attacks. Doubtless inconveniences will multiply in the effort to make normal life more secure, but the very best vengeance against terrorism is to live normally, not allowing a handful of madmen to deflect our choices and dictate our doings.

As to the perpetrators: here a different consideration applies. The hope of civilised society is premised on a refusal to overlook breaches of the fundamental contract aimed at enabling people to coexist. An act of terrorism, especially one involving murder of civilians, is vile in itself and an attack on the heart of that contract. The right vengeance is to bring the perpetrators before a court of justice and thereby oblige them to suffer the penalties of the contract they tried to destroy. The wrong response is to resort to meet terrorism with terrorism – for that also destroys the contract on which civilisation rests, and which is more important than present anger or past offences.

Capital Punishment

Those who are in favour of the death penalty have more affinity with assassins than those who are not.

REMY DE GOURMONT

It is a mistake to think that opponents of the death penalty are invariably sentimentalists, motivated by tenderness to those convicted of deliberate murder. They might, quite rightly, often be motivated by compassion for others branded as criminals, who in more rational, more just, or kinder dispensations would not be criminals at all – for example, prostitutes and drug addicts. They might also understand, although (a different thing) neither condone nor forgive, murder committed in the unmeditated grip of passion. Such attitudes are prompted by sympathy for the difficulties that can divert a life into making a hell for itself and others – or just for the frailties of the human spirit, so numerous and sometimes so final that they seem to be its destiny.

But it does not follow that opposition to capital punishment arises from sympathy for people who commit deliberate murder. Far from it. Deliberate murderers are contemptible scum, who kill not only their victims but a part of each member of their victims' families. They rob their victims of their futures, their relationships, their possibilities, throwing away whole worlds of existence in the split-second it takes to fire a gun or detonate a bomb. And they condemn the victims' families to a life sentence of consequences, staining their lives with a brutal mark they can never forget, even if they somehow come to assimilate the scarcely comprehensible truth that they have undergone a gratuitous, violent, horrifying loss of someone they loved and whose life was integral to their own. No accumulation of years effaces such a thing, and absolutely nothing excuses it.

In light of this, you would think that relatives of murder victims would be the first to cry revenge, and wish to see murderers put down like vermin and thrown into a hole. The thought of mass killers, bombers, murderers of children, makes the gorge rise in the throat, and invites only revulsion and contempt. Yet even from this point of view capital punishment is not the answer. There are many reasons why, but one is paramount. It has nothing to do with respect for the murderer, or his rights, or the supposed sanctity of his dangerous life. Rather, it has everything to do with respect for ourselves, and the kind of society we should strive to have. The point is simple: we should refuse to lower ourselves to a level anywhere near the murderer's own.

If the argument for capital punishment is the biblical one of an eye for an eye, then execution is no revenge. If a murderer lives as long as his victim's family, and suffers from life imprisonment in some way analogous to their lifelong sentence of loss, then a millionth part of revenge is served. But to kill a murderer not only pushes us in his moral direction, it merely shortens his suffering. When he is the calculating murderer of dozens or hundreds – a bomber of crowded buildings, for example, or of airplanes – releasing him from prison by death cannot compensate a billionth part for what he has done. Even for the vengeful, therefore, execution is no satisfaction. And yet it stains us in perpetrating it.

The capital punishment debate is complex because so many other considerations impinge. Why keep a murderer alive at society's expense? ask its supporters. The average lifer costs taxpayers nearly half a million pounds. What about rehabilitation and possible miscarriages of justice? respond opponents, on the grounds that it is easy to end a life, but impossible to recall it. And the sceptical ask, How can some simultaneously be pro-execution and anti-abortion, while others hold the reverse view? What if any are the differences between abortion, killing in war, and judicial executions, all legalised forms of killing?

This is a pertinent set of questions, and some are harder to answer than others. But the demand that we do not, in promoting our noblest ethical hopes, allow ourselves to mimic the actions of murderers clearly defined, says that whatever answers we give them, none defend capital punishment.

Bystanders

Disaster crushes one man now, afterward others.

EURIPEDES

If there are any bystanders left in the world – people on the sidelines, unaffected by major events of war, terrorism, global capitalism and technological change – they are very few. Inhabitants of remote Pacific islands or the forests of the Amazon might merit the description if they were not directly affected by environmental problems and the encroachment of commercial hunger for raw materials. Similarly, countries which claim neutrality are not really on no one's side, they are on everyone's side – as revealed by the fact that escaped Allied prisoners could find safety in Switzerland during the war against Nazism, while at the same time their pursuers could equally safely bank their money there.

But it is otherwise impossible for anyone now to stand aside from world affairs. It is an illusion to think that one can avoid the line of fire, or claim exemption from the effect of forces that smash and grind against each other internationally. Civilian populations are now front-line troops; they became so in the twentieth century's wars, suffering bombing and deprivation, their mobilisation in those immense struggles making them a target even in their homes, the aim being as much to unnerve as to kill them – for a demoralised enemy is as good as a defeated one.

Terrorism has exactly the aim, as its name implies, of frightening civilian populations into forcing their governments to concede. It takes only a few determined people to achieve this, applying the lesson – learned from the Spartans at Thermopylae via the Russian bands which harassed Napoleon's retreating Grand Armée, to the resistance fighters and insurgents everywhere in the modern world – that small forces can defeat big ones; in the case of whole populations, by means of psychological war.

Thus a well-directed terrorist attack is destructive far beyond its primary site; it can paralyse communications, clog the wheels of ordinary life, panic millions, wipe value off stock exchanges, destroy industries and thereby livelihoods – all as a function of purely psychological aftershock, whose effectiveness lies in its reaching ever further outward in space and time, radiating from the original focus, in some respects intensifying in the process.

Saying that there are no bystanders any more means that everyone is involved in everything. Even inaction is action; if you see someone injured and do nothing to help, you have acted negatively. There is a choice about one's manner of involvement: as witness, victim, fighter – for peace, and common sense; or as the kind who does physical battle, which is justified when it opposes greater evils – or as helper of the victims, since the only certainty is that there will always be victims.

Running away does no good, especially psychological and intellectual running away. This does not just mean refusal to face the fact that we all now live in some degree of physical danger, even in our ordinary lives in otherwise peaceful circumstances. It also means refusal to recognise, think through, and try to deal with, the sources of that danger – the sources of resentment, suspicion, hatred and finally conflict within and between peoples.

Among the main sources are these, and they are linked: disparities in wealth and power, and fundamental differences of culture, especially religious and moral culture. The link lies in the way wealth and power can, even if unintentionally, make poverty and weakness feel humiliated and therefore – in respect of its religious and moral culture – insulted. These inflame more concrete causes of opposition, such as exist in the Middle East, the Balkans and Ireland for more recent historical reasons. The mixture is always volatile, and the cants of nationalism, of the sacred, or (worst of all) both, are ever handy for whipping a dangerous minority into violent anger. The rest is tragedy.

This analysis implies the remedy, infinitely easier to state than effect. It is to make the world fairer, and to liberate it from the distorting influence of antiquated beliefs – at very least, by removing them from the public arena, allowing everyone there to be an individual human being rather than a label, and inviting our respect accordingly.

Slavery

Men would rather be starving and free than fed in bonds.
PEARL S. BUCK

At time of writing there are, by one measure, more slaves in the world than at any time in history: 27 million people all told, in forced labour camps, debt bondage, the sex industry, professional beggary, domestic servitude, and work – work without pay and under threat of violence, which is the definition of slavery – in agriculture, mining and factories. A very large proportion of them are children, many of whom are commercially trafficked.

In South Asia about a million children work unpaid in the hand-woven carpet industry from dawn until after nightfall, in horrible conditions. They are kept hungry so that they stay awake, and when rest is finally permitted they sleep on the floor next to their looms. They might be considered the lucky ones, given the yet greater numbers sold into prostitution or servitude, and even into bizarre and dangerous lives in the Arabian Peninsular as camel-jockeys.

Those who are enslaved by history – who dwell on past wrongs, who keep ancient conflicts and quarrels alive, who even seek reparations for the wrongs suffered by their ancestors – would do the world a greater service by turning their attention to present-day slavery instead. A concerted effort might open the gates of China's forced labour camps, free the Haitian sugar-plantation slaves, rescue the child prostitutes of Southeast Asia, and end the chattel slavery in Mauritania and the Sudan where slave markets still exist and where you can buy six children for one Kalashnikov.

Human history is the history of slavery. No great civilisation or empire has ever existed which was not built on the sweat of slaves. The institution of slavery once seemed entirely natural; it was defended by people as remote in time and outlook as Aristotle and Thomas Jefferson. The fact that it not only still exists but – in all its ugliness and evil – flourishes, is a staggering fact. And the problem is not helped but hindered by the retrospective claims of those who are the descendants of past slaves, for they devote their energies to demanding reparations instead of working to eradicate slavery from our present and future.

African-Americans are among those most determined to get compensation for the past. Who should pay them? The descendants of the warlike African tribes who hunted down less warlike Africans, and sold them to Arab merchants in Zanzibar and Egypt? Or the descendants of those Arabs? From the people in America, Europe and Russia (Pushkin's grandfather was thought to be an African slave in Moscow) who bought the slaves the Africans caught and the Arabs traded? Consider the history of the Yao, the East African Bantu who served as the Arab traders' 'hunting dogs' in enslaving great numbers of Amaravi in the African Rift. Should their descendants now be made to pay?

Most slaves taken to the Americas went in Portuguese, Spanish and British ships. To think that the peoples of those countries were of one mind in supporting slavery is quite wrong. In 1790 the twelve-year-old William Hazlitt found himself at the dinner table of a wealthy Liverpool resident whose fortune was made in slave-worked West Indian plantations. Hazlitt wrote home in disgust, 'The man who is a well-wisher to slavery is a slave himself.' Shall the descendants of those who strove for the abolition of slavery against that mightiest of foes, economic interest, be among the repayers? Why did (to choose one from many examples) Jesse Jackson demand that Britain should pay compensation, rather than thanking it for leading the way in efforts at abolition?

All of us probably have an ancestor who was a slave somewhere sometime in history, no matter what ethnicity and geography explains our antecedents; for slavery is an historical universal. We can therefore all demand apologies from one another for mankind's turpitudes. But it is better worth remembering that we poison the present by our self-imposed slavery to unforgivingness over offences of the past – and that this explains almost all conflicts, from Northern Ireland via the Balkans to Kashmir. That is a form of slavery which we desperately need to abolish too.

Experience

Experience is a comb nature gives to the bald.

CHINESE PROVERB

'Beware of entrance to a quarrel,' Polonius cautioned Laertes, 'but, being in, bear it that the opposed may beware of thee.' Less elegantly, Mao Zedong remarked that war is not crochet. In times of danger such counsel tends to be loudest, because it reminds us that hesitation, timidity, and insufficiencies of vigour and resources, invite catastrophe. Such are the lessons of experience.

But experience has even better lessons to teach. Wars eventually end, and when they do they result either in the defeat of all the parties, or the victory of all the parties. This is no paradox. To see why, compare the sequels to the First and Second World Wars. After the first, the 'victorious' nations imposed punitive reparations on defeated Germany. The economic disaster and resentment caused by this foolish policy, against which Keynes argued strenuously at the time, paved the way to resumption of global conflict within a mere twenty years. Thus, everyone lost. After 1946 the Marshall Plan was put into effect to reconstruct the countries devastated by the conflict. Rebuilding of cities, industrial investment, the provision of jobs, livelihoods, hope and self-respect for individuals, together with the imaginative and courageous vision of an integrated and co-operative Europe, resulted in everyone winning.

If this lesson were ever properly learned, real wars would begin when the concussion of missiles and miseries abates. This is the war of hearts, aimed at building friendship, repairing economies, cultivating mutual understanding and respect, fostering co-operation, binding people together by trade, educational and cultural exchanges, tourism and sport. It is harder to hate those you know than strangers in the mass whose ways seem queer or downright objectionable. The causes of most conflicts involve large admixtures of mutual ignorance, the parent of suspicion and hostility. To know is to understand, and to understand is far more often to tolerate than to condemn.

Everyone knows these lessons of experience: stated, they seem painfully obvious. But experience also teaches how infrequently they are heeded. Memory is short; peace and ease let the weeds of folly grow back. Ancestral voices prophesy (in the old sense of teach, not foretell) that if you hurt a person's affections and his pride, if you spit on his gabardine and tread on the crops he has sown to feed his family, you will turn him into a bitter enemy – and that it is sufficient if he only thinks you treated him so. How is it that these things nevertheless keep happening? Experience's greatest lesson, it would seem, is that the lessons of experience are too easily forgotten – or, which comes to the same, too late learned.

This explains the cynicism of the Chinese proverb quoted above, and Gide's observation that 'experience teaches only the good observer' – and that too often people look to it not to learn but merely to select what will bolster their own side of an argument. In other respects, when experience accumulates upon those who persistently ignore it, it eventually crushes them into defeat; and then truly it is like the stern lights of the ship which, in Coleridge's analogy, 'illumines only the track it has passed'.

The philosophy of experience is known as empiricism. Empiricism says that a concept is valid only if it is derived from, or is testable by, experience. The alternative theory is 'rationalism', the view that truth cannot be attained otherwise than by reasoning from self-evident first principles. The rationalist paradigm of knowledge is logic, the empiricist paradigm is science. Empirical knowledge is less certain than logic; it is tentative, responsive to new evidence and better research, always open to test. It is therefore the very embodiment of the spirit of preparedness to learn. Outside the formal disciplines of logic and mathematics there are no absolute certainties – except of course in religion, which abounds in them, to the extent that people commit murder for their sake. But the experience of history always shows the danger of dogma. What additional bitterness of experience is needed before we learn to return dogma to the kennels of history whence it came?

Grief and Remembrance

Suicide

He who saves a man against his will as good as murders him.

HORACE

It goes without saying that most cases of suicide are profoundly tragic occurrences, especially for families and friends left behind. In other cases – a minority – it is a blessing for those thereby released from suffering. Sometimes both points are true together. But it too often happens that suicide is prompted by the kind of psychological anguish – shame, sorrow, despair – which might in time, and with help, have abated. That is why the bereaved often feel guilt to an extraordinary degree, blaming themselves for failing the loved one at the time of danger.

They might also feel anger, when they experience the event as an act of rejection and selfishness. But it is rarely either. Leaving aside cases where death was not the intended outcome of what was really a plea for help, the desperation of the suicidal moment has to be immense for anyone to carry it through. In the face of that degree of agony, the only appropriate sentiment is sorrow that life reaches such passes for so many.

But suicide can be a kindly resource too. The agonies and indignities of hopeless illness might often be lessened by the love of companions and modern medicine. But if a person rationally chooses a quiet and painless death instead, to refuse him is not merely unjust but cruel. The debate over euthanasia has been won by the forces of sympathetic reason elsewhere – notably in the Netherlands – but in many places it remains obstructed by confused and misplaced beliefs about the 'sanctity of life' – an example of the way inhumanity so often masquerades as piety.

It is an oddity that those who invoke the sanctity of life are not as invariably opposed to war, arms manufacture and capital punishment as they are to euthanasia and abortion. Yet these latter are intended to help the living, while the former are designed to harm them. A proper sense of what makes death good or bad has to include this premise: that the quality of life is the sacred thing, not its mere quantity.

Although the mechanisms of disease and senescence can bring gentle endings to life, it too often happens that dying is a torment. In such cases not only the victim but the loving witnesses suffer. Contrast the case in which a person elects death before dying becomes too hard. He is able to say farewell, and to go with the painless ease that medical science now so simply provides. It is a devoutly wishable consummation.

Assisted suicide is the best form of euthanasia, for it has the elective participation of the subject. Involuntary euthanasia occurs when someone is unable to express a desire to die, but is in such a terrible state that a quick means of ending life is administered. There are many cases where both forms of euthanasia are justified. In jurisdictions where, nevertheless, euthanasia is illegal (even if widely practised; which is almost everywhere – for human pity is stronger than legalities), many are needlessly condemned to suffering by the chief anti-euthanasia argument: that murder might lurk under the cloak of kindness.

So indeed it might. But that is not a reason for letting unrelievable suffering continue. It is a reason instead for so arranging matters that abuse (everything, legal or otherwise, is open to abuse: humans are endlessly ingenious) is minimised.

Opponents of euthanasia imagine that inconveniently ageing parents will be destroyed like unwanted kittens; that hard-pressed hospitals will routinely clear beds by increasing morphine dosages not only in terminal cases but in doubtful ones too; that someone will ask for a last injection just weeks before some spectacular medical breakthrough. These anxieties cause the sum of human agony to mount in hospitals and nursing-homes everywhere.

The rule should be to allow euthanasia when it is obviously the right and merciful course. It is not beyond human wit to devise thoughtful procedures for determining the justifiability of candidate cases. There will be difficult cases; there could be mistakes; abuses might occur. But genuine acts of mercy, in which we help those urgent to escape suffering, indignity, or both, will justify us.

Loss

How easily life loses in a day what many years of toil and pain amassed.

PETRARCH

It is a grateful fact of human psychology that we forget our suffering. We do not forget that we suffered, but we do expunge the felt quality of the experience as it actually occurred. Life would be unbearable otherwise, beset by too-readily rekindled pain as sharp as its first appearance. Perhaps the agony of Borges' character Funes the Memorious, the man who could forget nothing, lay as much in his capacity to relive the raw quality of suffering as in the burden of his inability to erase millions of trivial memories.

But we do not forget our losses, because loss – especially of those we love, or of crucial places or things – reshapes our world, and obliges us to learn again the task of navigating it. Absence is a large presence; a gap in the familiar array of people who matter to us, or in the usual events which make the pattern of our lives, is a far bigger space than one imagined possible until it appears. For that reason bereavement, divorce, loss of a job, loss of a home – the major losses – are the most stressful and distressing of all experiences. And they can happen with such cruel suddenness that they make us lose other things besides: faith in the world, confidence in ourselves.

Common wisdom sees that a preparedness to lose is a necessary condition of gain. Naturally enough, most hope they can escape the condition, which makes loss more bitter when it occurs. It is hard to accept that to live is to lose, that to love is to lose, that trying to achieve anything of value is to lose – and that the only way to gain what matters is to accept these facts with courage.

It was against the devastating effects of loss that the Stoic philosophers of antiquity tried to arm people by their teachings, given the uncertainty of everything in life except the inevitability that we will lose some of what we most cherish. When we fall in love, for example, we do not think that we will one day lose the beloved; but so we will, as surely as the sun rises every day – through death at last, if our loves are deep; or through the mischances of growing apart, changing, finding new loves, losing old hopes, and accumulating too many misunderstandings. Such is life, and even the brightest optimist has to accept the fact.

Accordingly the Stoic thinkers advised their fellows to possess only what they would not mind losing. Montaigne learned from them to think as he did; he wrote, 'I love not to know an accompt of what I have, that I may less exactly feel my losses.' The point was an instance of the more general one that since we have little control over external events, we must learn to govern ourselves instead; the less we desire, the less we base our serenity or satisfaction on what happens outside us, and therefore the less our loss will be when the inevitabilities occur.

But although this teaching was designed to help people bear vicissitudes bravely, and in its inspiration is one of the tenderest and most thoughtful of philosophies, it misses a very important point. This is that if one is frugal with one's emotions – limiting love in order to avoid its pains, stifling appetites and desires in order to escape the price of their fulfilment – one lives a stunted, muffled, bland life only. It is practically tantamount to a partial death in order to minimise the electric character of existence –

its pleasures, its ecstasies, its richness and colour matched by its agonies, its wretchedness, its disasters and grief. To take life in armfuls, to embrace and accept it, to leap into it with energy and relish, is of course to invite trouble of all the familiar kinds. But the cost of avoiding trouble is a terrible one: it is the cost of having trodden the planet for humanity's brief allotment of less than a thousand months, without really having lived.

Obsequies

Lament not the dead but the living.

FULLER

If ever there were proof that our own deaths are no part of our lives, it is our funerals. We will not attend them, although we will be at their centre, and we will have nothing to do with them, though they are about us. Funerals exist for the living, to help the people left behind gather the realisation of loss, and go through a process which takes them from one life into another, the latter having in it new shapes and relationships configured by absence.

The best funerary traditions are those which aim at catharsis. In cultures where open-hearted expression of grief is acceptable, or where the mourners get drunk together, the excess acts like a lancet puncturing and emptying grief's first fullness. Nothing can or should substitute for the periods of returning sorrow which follow, nor the adjustment which takes time and cannot be forced; but the first stage of shock can be properly met and left if the act of parting is explicit, which is what a funeral is meant to be.

It is traditional for obsequies – funeral observances – to consist in praise of the departed, celebration of his gifts and achievements, recognition of his importance to family and friends, and acceptance of the pain his death causes. The ancients said, *De mortuis nil nisi bonum*, 'Say nothing but good of the dead.' The tradition is a good one, because although each of us is an alloy of secrets and bad habits, the owner of many regretted deeds and a long list of sins, we also, at our best, are capable of much human good, which those who care about us would like to emphasise and remember – because it helps them, and keeps the best part of us alive when mortality has removed all occasion for the exercise of our weaknesses.

Over-accentuating the positive has been tellingly challenged by Ambrose Bierce's remark that 'epitaphs show that virtues acquired by death have a retroactive effect.' It is often true that grief gilds, and sorrow sanctifies; and often true also, as la Rochefoucauld observed, that such obsequies are aimed at flattering the living relatives rather than the deceased. But this happens mainly at grand funerals, on state occasions, in Thespian wakes, and at the passing of celebrated poets and composers whose works transmute into monuments of genius at the touch of the reaper's blade. By contrast, in the ordinary funeral with its vast ordinary grief, the kind things said about the dead, and the good things he is remembered for, are a balm to the hurt of the living, and have a special meaning for them, because by singling out his virtues and consigning all else to silence, they are expressing their love.

In the *Iliad* Homer gives a detailed account of the obsequies of heroes, describing the preparations when he recounts the death of Patroclus, and the aftermath when he describes the funeral of Hector. When the body of Patroclus was brought back to his grief-stricken friend Achilles it was washed and anointed with oil, and its wounds were closed with ointment. His body was then covered with a linen cloth and a 'fair white robe'. All night long Achilles poured dust on his own head with both hands, and his men sat round him weeping.

After Hector's death at the vengeful hand of Achilles, the Trojans spent nine days building him a funeral pyre. On the tenth they lit it, and when the body had been consumed the flames were quenched with libations of wine; after which his bones were collected, wrapped in purple cloth, placed in a golden urn, and buried. Then the Trojans went back to Priam's palace to feast. 'Thus,' says Homer, 'did they celebrate the funeral of Hector, tamer of horses.' Both Greeks and Trojans were mighty speech-makers; but no speech is mentioned here by Homer.

These were the obsequies of heroes; but what inspired them was love and grief, as in almost every funeral held daily in our contemporary world.

Remembrance

At the going down of the sun, and in the morning,
We will remember them.

LAURENCE BINYON

Spartan mothers sent their sons to battle with the words, 'Return either with your shield, or on it' – meaning: come back victorious or come back dead. That was the spirit that made Diogenes the Cynic go about in the brilliant noon sunshine of Athens with a lit lantern, saying, 'I am looking for a man; I saw some boys in Sparta once', thereby drawing invidious comparisons.

Despite their robust attitudes, the mothers of Sparta certainly mourned when their sons came back on their shields. When men died on behalf of their own, especially in defending against an aggressor, they truly earned the right of remembrance, which is the utmost a community can offer those who gave themselves in its service. The opposite is no mere dereliction; to forget the gratitude owed to someone who put his body between you and the violence of an enemy is a culpable thing.

Such is the aim of Remembrance Day, to think of the young men (and women) who went with songs to the battle, 'straight of limb, true of eye, steady and aglow', as Binyon's 'For the Fallen' romantically claims. That poem, from which the League Ode is taken ('They shall not grow old, as we who are left grow old;/ Age shall not weary them, nor the years contemn;/ At the going down of the sun, and in the morning,/ We will remember them'), is moving and tender, and like many verses prompted by the monumental struggle of 1914–18 conveys with great richness the poetry and pity of war. It is engraved on thousands of memorials, which, with their flowers and solemnity, sanctify the sacrifice of hundreds of thousands of service personnel – a vast army, mainly of youth – lost in the silence of the past.

And there's the rub. This proper recollection of the dead of past wars has become an end in itself. But it should in addition be an instrument for a further and greater purpose, namely, to question war itself. Which wars in history were truly worth fighting? How did they start? Why, in general, do wars happen? What folly, greed, selfishness, madness, stupidity or wickedness causes them? How can a few fat old men who stay at home in offices send thousands of youths to be maimed and killed in the process of maiming and killing other youths? How can war ever be tolerated, still less glorified?

It is a platitude to say that the First World War – the source of Remembrance Day – should not have happened. People sentimentally remember its dead; they should also remember the waste and horror of that futile struggle which destabilised the world and brought decades of terrible suffering in the further wars, hot and cold, that sprang from it, like flies from the maggots in a corpse.

The Second World War was fought with justification by the Allies, but there was no justification for its source, which was the viciousness of a vile ideology. Remembrance Day should therefore also be about war's causes: ugly faiths, intolerance, lust for power and revenge, mutual hatreds prompted by historical accidents or differences of colour, custom or culture. It therefore also teaches that there are indeed times when aggression has to be countered, when bad people have to be stopped from doing worse, and when hard-won freedoms have to be defended against those who seek to impose barbarisms and oppressions in their place.

Remembrance Day has become a soft-focus event, a ritual laying of wreaths, a ceremonial marshalling of dignitaries, a parade of mutually hostile politicians temporarily pretending solidarity. Nevertheless it represents something honourable – an observance for those whose lives were shockingly abbreviated for their community's sake – but it misses the point if it does not also instigate a hard, penetrating look at war and the meaning of war, aimed at making the survivors resolute for peace, and as resolute in fighting when fighting is a genuinely necessary and unavoidable act of self-protection. Remembrance Day would in such circumstances be even more pointful – not least because it is what the dead of past wars thought they were dying for.

Nature and Naturalness

Naturalness

It were happy if we studied nature more in natural things.
PENN

Medical research suggests that gay male couples could have children. This seems repugnant to many for the vague reason that it seems to them 'unnatural'. They point to the fact that nature ensures the continuation of humankind by providing two sexes equipped in appropriately different ways for mingling their genes. Tampering with this arrangement, they say, is unnecessary and wrong. They also think it unnatural for children to have same-sex parents, arguing that their perception of human relationships will be distorted as a result. This objection already hampers the efforts of both male and female gay couples seeking to have children by adoption, surrogacy, or donor insemination.

Opposition to supposed unnaturalness in matters of sex has a long history. Not just homosexuality but any form of sexual activity that cannot lead to procreation has been so labelled. Catholic ethics regards masturbation as worse than rape because the latter might at least cause pregnancy, the possibility of which is the primary criterion of legitimate sex even in marriage – although doubtless that would still not be enough to make gay male parenthood acceptable. Traditional Protestant views were sometimes even more restrictive, at their extreme enjoining celibacy.

The crucial question is: what is natural? And if something is unnatural, does that automatically make it wrong? Reflection prompts surprising answers. For one thing, those who think 'nature' is a pseudonym for 'God' can be quickly disabused by noting that 'natural' is not a synonym of 'good', because plenty of natural things are not invariably good, such as diseases, earthquakes and untimely death. And many things once thought unnatural – vaccination, blood transfusion, organ transplants – are now regarded as good although unnatural; and perhaps some have even come to regard them as natural.

But the fact is that nothing is truly unnatural, because everything that exists, including human intelligence, is a product of nature. Human intelligence is as much a feature of the world as rain or grass, and the effects of its activity – dammed rivers, concrete cities, plastics, genetic modification of crops and animals (wheat and pet dogs are GM products of our earliest civilisation), destruction of species like the polio virus and the Bengal tiger – are natural in the same way as the effects of exploding volcanoes and biting mosquitoes. If human intelligence can devise ways for genes from two men to result in a child, their doing so is an entirely natural event.

Nor is there anything unnatural about nature working changes upon itself in the quest for advantages: the lion preys on the antelope, evolving teeth and strength to that end, while the antelope flees the lion, evolving alertness and swiftness to that opposite end. The human immune system and its viral and bacterial enemies are likewise equally parts of nature, each trying to do the best for itself in ways that can be fatal for the other side. And all this is wholly part of nature.

So, if it is not unnatural for two men to produce a child through human ingenuity, the conservative's question has to change focus, and ask instead: Is it natural for a child to be brought up by two men? This in effect is to ask whether same-sex parenting is acceptable, and it has to be answered not from the viewpoint of people who like things to happen as they have always happened in the past, but from the perspective of children of such parents. And here the answer is not surprising but simple.

We think it a good thing if children are loved and well-nurtured, living in a home with sufficient resources for their all-round welfare. What does it matter if a child lives in such a home with grandparents, or adoptive parents, or – as an example of a same-sex couple – two aunts? Sentiment prompts us to think that living with natural parents is best. Let us grant that it is, and ask: what does it matter if the child's natural parents are both male or both female?

At this point objectors claim that children need parents of different sexes so that they can learn about 'natural' human relationships. But this is a feeble argument as well as a question-begging one, the latter because it reverts to using 'natural' as a commendatory term. To answer it one need only ask, Is it impossible for children to learn about human relationships, in all their variety, if they have only one parent? No. Why then should it be so if they have two but of the same sex? They can see the wider community around them, and can compare their own families with others, exactly as children do who live with more than one differently sexed parent.

Moreover, the supposedly traditional nuclear family of mother, father and two-and-a-half children is neither the dominant model in our society, nor is it even truly traditional. Extended families, one-parent families, multiply rearranged families full of step-siblings and half-siblings of all ages, are just as common. Human nature and affections are protean and living; individuals relate in all sorts of ways, and although certain relationships might be thought preferable to others, and although others do obvious harm, it is invidious to say which of the rest are 'normal' or 'right'. In the larger picture, the fact that a child's parents are the same sex as each other is no more nor less relevant than the fact that a child will usually be the same sex as at least one of its parents. The crucial point is the well-being of the child, which has very little to do with the ages, sexes, or actual genetic relationship between the child and his carers, and everything to do with his being loved and nourished.

People use 'natural' and 'unnatural' as emotive terms expressing their preferences. What is considered natural and acceptable in some cultures is thought disgusting in others, and at certain times in history what is considered natural is for that reason despised – as at the end of the nineteenth century, when the rich ate white bread and sugar because whiteness denotes purity, with all the unpleasant natural bits 'refined' away, whereas now people eat brown bread and sugar because brown is the colour of health and shows that the foodstuffs are closer to their natural origins. With such changes of fashion and use affecting it, the concept of 'naturalness' is practically useless.

Nature

Nature is no spendthrift, but takes the shortest way to her ends.
EMERSON

Fragile human life often finds itself confronting nature's larger gestures – earthquakes, volcanoes, hurricanes, floods, droughts, pestilences and plagues, even fiery meteors from space. Nevertheless we choose to assume that, generally speaking, nature's ordered and law-like ways are benign. The power of natural disasters is a reminder that they are not; a few mighty and remorseless seconds of geophysics are enough to show that however securely men build, their shelters will never withstand nature.

In India the cause of earthquakes is also the cause of the Himalayas' height. Those stupendous mountains mark the border between the Indian and Eurasian tectonic plates, two of the giant scales forming the earth's crust. The Indian plate is moving slowly northwards, at a few inches a year – the same speed as human fingernails grow – converging with the southern edge of the Eurasian plate and lifting it. Everest is therefore the index of a monumental collision taking place more slowly than human senses can register – until, that is, stresses in the crust underfoot are released, and plate tectonics is revealed as a Samson bringing the temple of our certainties down around our ears.

Millions of tiny earthquakes happen daily, almost all of them too minor to detect. Newcomers to Japan are disconcerted to notice palpable tremors every few hours, until habituation prompts disregard. That is a pity, for continued awareness might keep one alert to the frailty of human tenancy among nature's indifferent forces. But the tendency is for people not really to believe that disaster might suddenly strike, even if they live right on a notorious tectonic edge or under a smoking volcano. They subconsciously think: there are things to do, people to meet, tasks to fulfil: how could life not go according to reasonable plan – which includes nature behaving itself? Such is the frame of mind of many who live along the San Andreas Fault in California, or in the hurricane belt of the southern United States, or along the low banks of Bangladesh's rivers.

At the same time, nature is as unyielding in defending itself as it is in exploding our expectations. A man is frail when a mountain falls on him; but give him the slimmest chance of survival – for example, a fissure to crawl into as an escape from the engulfing rock – and he will survive. This illustrates the tenacity of life, which Schopenhauer described as an instance of the general metaphysical will underlying all things – the determined struggle for continuance. Schopenhauer thought that the will to exist is a bad thing, because it pointlessly perpetuates suffering. But others are not so pessimistic, and redescribe nature's neutrality as even-handedness. 'Why should we fear to be crushed by savage elements,' Emerson asked, 'we who are made up of the same elements?'

People who enjoy opportunities for reflection – for which leisure is a condition; and a condition for leisure, in turn, is wealth, or at least freedom from necessity – tend to occupy areas of the world with temperate climates, fertile soil, and low frequencies of natural disasters. For them, nature is an amenity and an enjoyment: blossom-filled woods in spring, sandy beaches in summer, sparkling snows at Christmas, are not matters of life and death, but aesthetic delights instead. Nature in these guises elicits poems and songs, watercolour paintings and afternoon walks. No one writes an ode to a tsunami, or strolls in a storm – though he might, like Turner, paint one. It was a Romantic affectation to seek out the sublime and awful in nature; poets took pains to be overwhelmed by Alpine chasms and brooding forests. Such is the mental mark of urban civilisation. Rural civilisation is never so impressed. The shepherds who graze their sheep in Alpine chasms find them much less amazing than a city street. For them, nature – earthquakes and all – is merely natural; neither especially beautiful nor especially significant.

To view nature aesthetically, and even romantically, is better than to view it with such workaday indifference, because then it retains its power to refresh the town-wearied spirit which prompted Wordsworth to complain, 'Getting and spending we lay waste our powers/ Too little we see in nature that is ours.' But the romance requires a tincture of realism to take account of the truth in Turgenev's observation that 'Nature cares nothing for our human logic; she has her own, which we do not acknowledge until we are crushed under her wheel.'

Monsters

He who would fight monsters must take care not to become one.
NIETZSCHE

What is meant by labelling something 'unnatural' or 'grotesque', and calling it a monster? Behind news from Loch Ness – where periodic sightings of a strange creature are reported, and where repeated scientific expeditions never find anything – is the true meaning of that last word. It is a meaning that lurks as elusively as Nessie herself amid the distractions of legend and anecdote. From denoting any creature which is strange in appearance, usually huge, and terrifying, 'monster' is readily adapted to name a person who is cruel, wicked, or ugly. These juxtapositions of concepts are interesting in their own right – why is hugeness terrifying? Why is ugliness so readily associated with evil? – precisely because they are not accidental. But the key lies in what makes anything seem strange, misshapen or threatening in the first place. The explanation is: unfamiliarity.

In early maps, oceans were represented by blanks inscribed 'Here be monsters.' The phrase summarised sailors' reports of great weird beasts, Leviathans which lifted the sea on their backs and made the sign of the devil as they plunged into the deep. Even more numerous were the smaller but no less uncanny creatures we now know as manatee and dolphin, seal, eel and turtle. To the astonished eye of their first European beholders such apparitions – so deformed, strange and powerful – were too extraordinary to bode good.

In their reaction to these manifestations of the unfamiliar, early mariners displayed a common feature of the human psyche. Consider the ubiquity and centrality of monstrous beings in myth, art, literature and film. The modern popular imagination of the West is haunted by ghosts, vampires, were-wolves, Dr Frankenstein's monster, curse-inflicting Egyptian mummies, zombies, and aliens which invade and inhabit human flesh. These are the various descendants of Grendel, the beast of Beowulf, and the weird and fearsome creatures fought by Arthur's knights on their quests. The game is given away in Langland's *Piers Plowman*: the monsters there are incarnations of Sloth and Gluttony, Lust and Avarice, revealing them to be embodiments of our sins, our fears, our inner darkness. If there are no whales or crocodiles to serve as the pegs we hang our terrors on, we make others up instead, needing to externalise them in order to confront them.

Bruno Bettleheim hypothesised that fairy stories are ways of teaching children the hard facts of life in acceptable form. Hansel and Gretel are abandoned by their parents in the dark wood – allegorising parental death – where they encounter the witch in her house made of confectionery – allegorising the temptations and dangers of life – and so on: the interpretations are obvious, and apply illuminatingly to almost all the familiar tales. Monster stories are therefore for older children and adults what fairy stories are for younger children; allegorisations of everything hard to face but harder to escape.

As one would expect, this is most clearly visible in classical mythology, that treasure-house of psychological insight. Cerb-erus, the Chimera, Lamia, Medusa, the Hydra, the Minotaur – each of them a mixture of fierce beasts, and most having ser-pents, the icons of evil, as part of their bodies or hair – represent different aspects of the struggle people have with the two great intransegencies pitted against them: themselves, and the world.

Some interpreters think the Hydra story is an example of the latter. The Hydra was a huge hundred-headed serpent, which grew two new heads for each one it lost, as Hercules discovered when he fought it. On this interpretation, the Hydra symbolises the great marsh of Lerna, which defied all attempts to drain it by promptly drowning reclaimed land with new springs. *Hydor*, appropriately, is ancient Greek for 'water'.

Psychological monsters are extensions of sailors' monsters, frightening unfamiliars of unknown regions. They are the most characteristic expression of humanity's universal fear of whatever is anomalous or unusual. A salient example is the Old Testament's 'abominations'. Ancient zoology identified three classes of creatures: feathered birds, furred quadrupeds, and scaly fish – and therefore Israel was forbidden to eat anything which failed to fit those categories neatly, such as snakes, rodents with their human-like hands, sea-dwellers without scales, and pigs because they have the wrong kind of feet.

But once a monster is found a place in the scheme of things, it ceases to be monstrous and becomes natural. Consider whales, those immense and once-terrifying seigneurs of the deep. As objects now of affection and concern, the only monstrous thing associated with whales is mankind's cruelty towards them.

Madness

Men are so necessarily mad, that not to be mad would be another form of madness.

PASCAL

In one collective form of insanity, whole populations of people rise from sleep at about the same time each day, move in great herds to locations at some distance from their home territory, perform repetitive manoeuvres there, return home when evening falls, slump in front of a flickering coloured light, and after a while fall asleep again. They repeat the process day after day for decades. The disease is called 'normal life', and variations from it are regarded as eccentric; if the variations are marked enough they are even called 'madness' and 'delusion'.

This thought is intended to show that what counts as abnormal is a relative matter. 'All the world is queer, except me and thee,' the Quaker saying has it, 'and even thee is a bit odd at times.'

Human minds are weird things. On the standard and well-attested view of contemporary science, this is wholly a matter of physiology: the delicate wiring and chemistry of the brain is so complex, and its activities so finely balanced, that any number of things can upset it. No 'ghost in the machine' hypothesis is required to explain such mental bizarreries as Cotard's syndrome, whose victim believes that parts of his own body, or parts of the world, have disappeared; or Tourette's syndrome, whose sufferers involuntarily shout obscenities; or Koro, a widespread hysterical phenomenon occurring chiefly among East Asians, in which young men believe their genitals are shrivelling away or retracting irrecoverably into their abdomens. There are fixations, obsessions, mass delusions and any number of mental aberrations which in the view of contemporary psychiatry are mostly explainable on the basis of human biology. The view does not stop there: belief in spirits and homeopathy, and such apparently common phenomena as sexual jealousy and musical giftedness, can be set alongside such phenomena as multiple personality disorder and schizophrenia, to suggest that all these things occupy the same spectrum – and that all are therefore in some sense part of the 'normal' range of human curiosity, if properly seen in the light of medical science.

Most discussion of madness and other strange mental symptoms tends not to set them alongside, say, Munchausen syndrome and the sublimatedly sexual ecstasies of saints, presumably because a dividing line has to be found between what is psychologically 'normal' and 'abnormal' in order to make sense of either notion. What is refreshing about the no-nonsense, pragmatic, healthily scientific attitude, is its seeing the mind as a highly various thing, capable of swinging far beyond the commonplace in a variety of colourful and surprising ways.

One of the most curious of psychological phenomena is 'mass hysteria'. Many irrational beliefs and occurrences such as dancing mania – tarantella or St Vitus's Dance – are now often described as manifestations of mass hysteria. In the latter instance, it was once believed that if one had been bitten by a tarantula one could avert death by frenzied dancing. Epidemics of mad dancing swept Europe, noticeably in the seventeenth century; huge crowds of whirling gesticulating people danced for as long as possible, some falling dead from exhaustion. Some of the early epidemics started when a single person was bitten by a spider, his dance thereupon proving rapidly contagious. The last known outbreaks occurred in the early twentieth century. Mass hysteria appears to be a common occurrence in closed communities such as monasteries, prisons and (especially) girls' boarding schools; in the latter, stressful behaviour or panic in a high-status individual – a head prefect or favourite mistress – can trigger general upheaval.

An intriguing aberration is 'fugue', amnesiac wandering of the kind Agatha Christie once famously suffered. The victim sets off on a journey, seemingly purposeful and conscious, but actually in an altered, self-forgetful state of mind, travelling impulsively and directionlessly, perhaps across whole continents – and then 'wakes' in astonishment to find himself far from home, having in the meantime behaved very uncharacteristically. According to recent studies, there is no such thing as fugue considered as a separate mental disease; non-conscious wandering can be caused by brain injury and a variety of illnesses. But the majority view is that fugue is a choice that a stressed mind makes to escape one or another kind of intolerable situation, as if it wished to seek a better life.

'As if it wished to seek a better life' – perhaps philosophy is the sanest and most rational form of fugue we know.

Madness is supposedly the ultimate in human psychological unnaturalness. It is fascinating to study because it permits everything that the human condition offers in the way of comedy, tragedy, profundity and irreverence, and thereby yields insights which we would not willingly be without. Sanity needs madness for its own survival, and ordinarily sane folk seek temporary forms of its pleasanter manifestations accordingly, from the mild euphoria of parties and dancing to the non-sane states induced by alcohol, cocaine and other consciousness-altering substances. This permits the usually sober mortgage-paying commuter to leave his world of straight lines and fly about like a released balloon in several directions at once – giving him a moral holiday, a release and a refreshment for his cramped sane soul.

But more serious states of non-sanity can be painful to the sufferer, and they are disruptive to society, so society has to respond. We cannot leave the victim of inner torments without succour, nor can we have madmen driving about the public highways, operating complicated machinery, or looking after children. Once, when the world was simpler and communities more enclosed, a madman could be tolerated, even venerated as someone set apart by the gods. But the fabric of the social world has grown too fine and complex for anything flailing or disoriented to be let loose in it, threatening to tear its delicate strands.

But what is madness? We have been taught (by Laing, Foucault and others) to be suspicious even of our best medical judgements about what is 'normal' in the realm of mind, and we know that madness is not one thing but many. No longer tolerating the village idiot is one way in which perceptions of insanity have changed, but only one: for over the course of time madness has been redefined many times, both as regards its nature and its sources. Almost the only way to understand the shifting perceptions of madness through history is by looking for clues in literary texts and the history of medicine.

Foucault's influence has been much felt in this field of enquiry. He saw madness as created by attitudes, specifically those of the class which had the power to decide who counted as sane and who not. This view expressly opposes any which states that theories of madness address something objectively real in the world, namely, inner disturbances of mind which infect and disrupt the subject's relationship with others and the world around him. On this latter 'realist' view, even though the concept of madness is a product of how we think and talk (our 'discourse') about physical, social and psychological phenomena, nevertheless it is not a mere artefact of that discourse, not a mere fiction of our efforts at interpretation.

The realist's point is a good and sane one; but of course it merely reinforces the need to look with an especially judicious eye at the way insanity has been understood and accommodated by different societies in history, in order to see – by looking through the different faces of the prism thus offered – the object of the enquiry more clearly. As suggested, this fascinating and important project might best be conducted by sampling sources in cultural history, from Homer to the present by way of medieval sagas, Chinese poetry, Indian epics, Shakespeare and Cervantes, the German romantics, and more recent literary and medical treatments of madness. There are very rich pickings in this material. Take for example madness as presented in the literature of classical antiquity. Consider Dionysus, Bacchus, the Maenads, the Corybantes, the mass of portrayals in plays by Aeschylus, Sophocles and Aristophanes, the doctrine of humours in Hippocratic medicine – together with famous individual instances: the judgement of Polyphemus's neighbours when he told them that No-one had blinded him, Odysseus's feelings as he struggled against his bonds on hearing the Sirens' song – where might one stop?

The ancient gods tormented and rewarded with ecstasies, madness was a route to wisdom and prophecy, those mad with grief tore their hair and garments – any account of the notion, the practice, and the meaning of madness in antiquity would garner richly among these harvests. And that would mark just a beginning; for the rest of history has been as mad, and as full of madness, as its beginning; and still is.

One thing to be learned from looking for madness in history is how common it is – therefore, how commonplace, how ordinary; how, so to say, natural it is. This is another example of the natural place of the unnatural in the world, suggesting that it is in our scheme of things, and not in what it schematises, that the unnatural has its most natural place.

Clones

Man hath all which Nature hath, but more,
And in that More lies all his hopes of good.
MATTHEW ARNOLD

Something disquieting lurks among the predictable arguments
on either side of the cloning debate. On the one hand, the
biomedical advances underlying cloning are welcomed as
another great step towards the alleviation of human suffering.
On the other hand there is the standard chorus of horror and
alarm to the effect that mankind is interfering with nature,
usurping the prerogatives of God, and undermining the sanctity
of life.

With the rejoicing one wholeheartedly concurs. In response
to those who would rather see existing human beings suffer
than to see a tiny clutch of cells adapted to ending that suffering,
a speaking silence should suffice. But the disquieting fact is
that even those working towards therapeutic cloning, thereby
offering an immense boon to humanity's future, are eager to say
that they aim only to produce stem cells for research, and have
no intention of cloning humans. This defensiveness yields too
much to the ignorance and prejudice of the opposition.

For what is wrong with cloning humans? It is nothing other
than to produce a twin. Is there anything unnatural or evil about
twins? Think of a couple denied children by the husband's
sterility. Is it better that his wife should be impregnated by a

male stranger via a glass tube than that they should produce a child wholly hers – technically her twin but in all other social and emotional respects their child to love and nourish? Might not a child who is the product of donor insemination wonder who her 'real' father is, and be troubled by ignorance of her origins? In the cloning case she would have no such anxieties.

The nonsense people talk about cloning stems from the prison-cell of religious belief. Pious exclamations about the sanctity of life, and about not interfering with God's purposes, conceal a farrago of confusion. Life's sanctity resides in its quality, not its mere quantity, for there is nothing sacred in suffering. And if we were to 'avoid interfering with God's purposes' we would not use penicillin, nor raise money for the Third World's starving, nor build a roof over our children's heads (which, as it happens, Jesus instructed us not to – 'consider the lilies of the field' – but not even Christians are foolish enough to obey).

If there is a deity of the kind imagined by votaries of the big mail-order religions such as Christianity and Islam, and if this deity is the creator of all things, then it is responsible for cancer, meningitis, millions of spontaneous abortions every day, mass killings of people in floods and earthquakes – and too great a mountain of other natural evils to list besides. It would also, as the putative designer of human nature, ultimately be respons-ible for the ubiquitous and unabatable human propensities for hatred, malice, greed, and all other sources of the cruelty and murder people inflict on each other hourly.

Some among us are disgusted by the thought of such a thing in the universe, and are mightily glad that the arguments alleging the existence of anything like it are nugatory, having the same intellectual respectability as arguments about the existence of fairies. But alas there are plenty of folk who believe in supernatural agencies, and who therefore have to believe either that earthquakes and meningitis are our own fault –

perhaps because we do insufficient amounts of obeying and worshipping to please the gods – or that these evils are somehow for our good. Either excuse is risible.

Such folk, in resisting medical advances, would leave man's sufferings to the tender mercies of the inventor of cancer and earthquakes. But the truth is that the fate and well-being of mankind is our own responsibility, and happily – despite all the turpitude weighed against it – the world contains enough human intelligence and kindness to offer fragments of hope for the future. In promising to cure some of the most dreadful afflictions we or those we love might suffer, biomedical research stands high among those hopes.

Decay

Apples taste sweetest just as they begin to rot.

SENECA

Books that make you see the world differently are rare enough to merit celebration when they appear. One of these is a book about death and decay by a popular Dutch biologist-essayist-broadcaster called Midas Dekkers, a man of infinite jest and wisdom who, like Yorick before him, knows that all must come to dust, and revels in the fascination, beauty and horror of how it happens. What he gives us is the story of time and change in the processes of nature – or, more bluntly: the story of ageing, decay and death.

If you were not a vegetarian or a Parsee before reading Dekkers, or a woman, a microbe, or a cockroach, you will quite likely wish to be at least one of them by the time you finish his book. If you want to live long, be a woman. If you do not want to be interred in the cold soil nor committed to the flames when you die, be a Parsee, and have a grave in the sky atop a Tower of Silence. If you desire an ancestry that predates the dinosaurs, be a cockroach. And if you wish to be more successful and various than any other creature on the planet, be a microbe, and help in the universal process of turning things into other things, which is what decay is all about.

Ageing in humans happens fastest in babies, Dekkers tells us, and slowest in the old. But most of your body is no older than a baby's body anyway, even if you are a nonagenarian, for the body constantly renews itself. It is just that the older you get, the less efficiently the body does so – until finally it switches the process off, and dies.

We do not eat 'fresh' meat, Dekkers points out, but rotting meat, for only carrion is soft enough to cook and eat. Water, says Dekkers, is one of the most destructive substances on earth; almost everything dissolves in it, including buildings and mountains. Air is no better, especially the oxygen in it, which rusts even the human body. Like the food we eat, water and air are as necessary to life as they are destructive of it.

Among the most fascinating and wittily presented facts are those relating to human death – which is quite hard to achieve, apparently, unless the body is itself ready to do it – and subsequent disposal. We vaguely know about worms and crematoria – but what really happens? And why was there controversy over cremation, a method once reserved for atheists, witches and sodomites? In describing how nature disposes of corpses Dekkers takes us on a vertiginous journey. The description given of a decomposing mouse in the essay on meat earlier in this collection draws on Dekker's description of the processes – and the microbes – involved in integrating a corpse into the world around it. Instincts of self-preservation make us nauseated when we encounter flesh too decayed – but the process is simply one of transfer, the reverse of turning the world around us into ourselves by eating it. In either direction the processes of digestion are nothing other than the ceaseless pulse of things entering into and leaving each other's natures.

One might dislike the idea of a rotting mouse's cheesy smell, but the account Dekkers gives is not invariably stomach-churning. A large part of his point is that what we see as decay, rottenness, collapse and demise, is a condition for the renewal of life, and also its fulfilment. Autumn is a case in point: the time when all the riches of the world offer themselves, so that ripening fruit (ripening and rotting are the same thing, distinguished only according to taste) and falling leaves are marks as much of bounty as of endings – of the promise of new beginnings as well as of completion.

A profound comment on death and life is offered by Bartok's ballet *The Miraculous Mandarin*. A gang of thieves employs a prostitute to lure men to their den, where they kill and rob them. One of the chosen victims is a Mandarin, who, when the girl dances seductively before him, conceives an overwhelming desire for her. The thieves try to kill him by poison and stabbing, but (like Rasputin) he refuses to die. They try hanging him from a lantern, but he and the lantern crash to the floor, where he begins to glow an unearthly green. All the while his burning eyes remain fixed on the girl. She understands, and takes pity on him, and accepts his embraces; and as soon as his desire for her is sated, his wounds begin to bleed, and he dies.

This tale goes to the heart of things.

Reading and Thinking

The Essay

English literature is rich in the art of the essay, which contains some of its greatest treasures. Essays are the perfect vehicles for discussion of anything; miscellaneous and catholic in subject and style, they afford readers not just pleasure but a broad supplementary education. The great age of the essay was the eighteenth and nineteenth centuries, but it began in English in the seventeenth century with Francis Bacon and – despite the hurry of contemporary journalism and the desiccation of contemporary academicism – still flourishes.

Any piece of non-fiction prose shorter than a book and longer than a note might count as an essay if, in addition, it has at least a touch of that indefinable and elusive thing, 'literary quality' – which means: either a natural or a conscious application of the power and beauty of language to effect choicer communication. Scientific papers and even business reports might display such quality, but more often they neither have nor aspire to it, and therefore do not count as essays.

For three centuries after Shakespeare's time essays and poetry constituted the two major genres of our literature. They were taken far more seriously than either novels or plays. Novels were regarded as an inferior form, at best a mere diversion for idle folk and at worst a corrupter of morals, until they began to gain respectability in the nineteenth century. Plays were something seen on stage, not read on the page; and they too were regarded as morally suspect, for theatres were places of assignation and romantic intrigue, conducted in the dim light of the auditorium against the barely-noticed background activity on stage.

It is easy to understand the essay's long supremacy as literature's chief prose form. Essays are supremely flexible and accommodating devices. They can be short or long, whimsical or serious, but they are always perfect as vehicles for experiment in style and ideas. They can entertain, instruct, surprise, provoke and delight, by the very fact of their miscellaneous nature and plasticity of structure, which allows their authors to take any route to any goal. Perhaps the closest thing today to the 'familiar essay' – the intimate, informal essay random in topic and design – is the newspaper 'column', where the columnist's personality and style are the main point.

But the essay's roots lie in more consciously literary soil: in classical antiquity, with the orations of Demosthenes and Cicero, the discourses of Plutarch and Epictetus, and the epistles of Seneca and Pliny the Younger. When Michel de Montaigne in the late sixteenth century adapted these models to create a miscellaneous and discursive instrument for exploring himself and his experience, he inaugurated the essay in its modern form. By describing them as 'attempts' or 'forays' – in French, *essaies* – he also gave them their modern name.

Montaigne's essays were immediate best-sellers, and within a few years of his death had been rendered into English by John Florio. But even before Florio began work on his influential translation, Montaigne was read in his native tongue by the philosopher Francis Bacon, who instantly saw the essay's potential. Bacon's first essays were published six years before Florio's Montaigne appeared, and he too found an appreciative readership hungry for more. He published three collections in his lifetime, and soon had imitators, the best among them Abraham Cowley.

From then until the early decades of the twentieth century the essay remained an immensely popular form. Its high period lay between 1710 and 1890 – from Addison and Swift near the end of Queen Anne's reign, to Robert Louis Stevenson and Matthew Arnold near the end of Queen Victoria's reign. Its golden age, coming at the mid-point of this span, was the creation of the two greatest masters in the genre: William Hazlitt and Charles Lamb, who in their different ways raised the essay to the peak of its form as an art.

The essay has now largely been absorbed by journalism and academia, in neither of which is it regularly viewed as an especially literary form. Journalism has shortened and popularised the essay, academia has lengthened and jargonised it, so the true essay is now a rarer commodity, and a somewhat highbrow one. But it still exists, and has some fine contemporary exponents, among them Gore Vidal, Joan Didion and Jonathan Raban.

It is no accident that the major period of the essay's flourishing, beginning with Addison and Steele, should happen when it did. England was then emerging from the revolutions of the seventeenth century, and from the Irish and French wars of William's and Anne's reigns, with a political settlement and a growing empire that inaugurated a long prosperous peace. In the same period the English language had become, in the hands of Newton, Locke and others, a marvellously serviceable instrument for discussion of things that matter – politics, manners, philosophy, science and history. A comparison of the baroque effusions of Sir Thomas Browne with the lucidity and grace of Addison shows how rapidly English prose matured in less than a century. Its new fitness matched the needs of a population growing in literacy and independent-minded curiosity about the world. Readers wished to be instructed and entertained, and the writers who responded found in the essay a form, and in vernacular English a language, wonderfully apt for the task.

Montaigne's essays never conform to their titles but wander informally and perceptively from one subject to another, bringing fresh ideas constantly into view. The English essayists felt the same freedom, and the itinerant, speculative nature of their work is reflected in the titles of the publications they founded to house it: *The Tatler, The Spectator, The Rambler, The Lounger, The Observer*. When Chalmer's *British Essayists* was published in 1808 it ran to forty-five volumes, nothing less being enough to embody two centuries' worth of treasures.

When Chalmer's volumes appeared Hazlitt and Lamb were young men. They had both already published books, but were only just beginning to write essays. The time was ripe; dozens of periodicals existed, there was a new Romantic spirit abroad in literature, and the age was one of violent party strife. People could take refuge from the tumult of the times in Lamb's charming whimsicalities, or they could grapple with it in the relish and power of Hazlitt's beautiful prose. No one had written like either of them before, and years later Robert Louis Stevenson remarked, 'We think we are very fine fellows nowadays, but none of us can write like Hazlitt.'

Stevenson had in mind Hazlitt's 'familiar essays', the perfect exemplars of what the essay could be. They have become classics of our literature. In one of them Hazlitt tells of his first encounter with the friends of his youth, Coleridge and Wordsworth, who later became his enemies. In another he describes the great Fives player, John Cavanagh; in a third he recounts a bare-knuckle prize-fight on the Berkshire Downs, watched by a vast crowd, on which bets amounting to three hundred thousand pounds had been laid; in a fourth he describes Poussin's painting of blind Orion, staggering to meet the dawn; and in a fifth, a sixth – in dozens more, all brilliant – he discusses art, theatre, books, politics and the human condition, always with extra-ordinary eloquence and insight.

Hazlitt wrote for the greatest periodical of the day, the *Edinburgh Review* under its redoubtable editor Francis Jeffrey. In the length and seriousness of its contributions Jeffrey's *Review* set a pattern for the highbrow Victorian periodicals which followed, boasting George Eliot, John Stuart Mill, Macaulay, Carlyle, Matthew Arnold and other great literary and philosophical names of the century among their contributors. At the same time a lighter style of essays flourished, aimed at amusing and entertaining rather than advancing thought, from Thackeray's 'Yellowplush Papers' in the mid-century to Hilaire Belloc's several 'On Nothing' volumes after the First World War.

By this time the essay was such a pillar of literature that reading and writing essays formed a central part of the school curriculum. There is no better proof of its enduring influence than the fact that one of the principal pedagogical collections, Peacock's *Selected English Essays*, was reprinted twenty-two times between 1903 and 1930.

In collections like Peacock's, generations of school children met Dr Johnson, Thomas de Quincey, Isaac Disraeli, Leigh Hunt, as well as those already mentioned. They read essays so that they could learn to write well and think straight, and they acquired a broad additional education in the process. Essays open windows into the past and other minds, so it gave these generations of students an unparalleled opportunity to expand their understanding of what lies beyond themselves and the present.

The essayists of the past are not studied in schools as they once were, but they are still read with relish and enjoyment, even if only by a minority. Wherever there is enjoyment of fine prose and agile thought, the names of Hazlitt, Addison and others of the great tradition survive, and the sheer quality of their achievement guarantees that they always will.

Reading and Reviewing

When critics disagree, the artist is in accord with himself.
WILDE

Cynics ascribe the popularity of book reviews to the laziness of those who want to know about new books without the fatigue of reading them, perhaps in order to appear knowledgeable at cocktail parties. No doubt there are such folk; but it is a safe bet that book reviews are popular for at least two dozen reasons besides, not least among them being – odd as it may seem – a genuine interest in books.

One reason that the old cliché about teaching ('those who can, do; those who cannot, teach') is not adaptable to book reviewing is that all reviewers are, *ipso facto*, writers, and many if not most are also authors. Still, a certain suspicion attaches to the enterprise of reviewing, as if it is neither quite a serious nor quite a worthy endeavour – definitely subordinate to the main task, frequently cheap in the doing and the result, and invariably parasitic – 'a louse on the locks of literature', in Tennyson's phrase.

To prove that this is palpably untrue of fiction reviewing one need only consider, say, James Wood or Michael Hofmann, to be reminded that one of the principal tasks of criticism, namely, to offer intelligent, informed, perceptive responses, continues to be well done by the best, even if sheer numbers both of books and 'books pages' in newspapers and magazines sometimes now adulterates what is otherwise on offer.

The older, more various and no less demanding avocation of non-fiction reviewing invites the same judgement, not least because it has a rich resource to draw upon in the expertise of those who can debate merits from a vantage of knowledge – historians, scientists, classicists, medical practitioners, philosophers and journalists. But noticing this brings into focus a startling fact: that the practice of contemporary reviewing, whether of fiction or non-fiction, owes nothing to self-styled 'critical theorists', those succubi of English Literature departments whose jargonings are read (if they are read at all) only by one another, and who have contributed nothing to the wider world since they hijacked the academic study of literature from its original Quiller-Couchian purpose: which was to educate, liberate, and civilise.

The reason is that the professionalisation of the academy has diverted its form of criticism away from engagement with life. In historic terms the difference is represented by Hazlitt and Coleridge: 'there is no greater critic than Hazlitt in any language ... he is the critic's critic as Spenser is the poet's poet', George Saintsbury wrote, before the twentieth-century turn to academic criticism – whose source, as David Bromwich perceptively remarks, is not Hazlitt but Coleridge, and which, in making and continually widening the gulf between 'the world of journalism, where new literature is fostered or starved, and the world of scholarship, where old literature is interpreted and canonised', is not concerned with taste, but with technique; not with the common readers' response to books and their connection with life as lived, but with specialist academic interest in methods and classifications, schools and '-isms', unconscious influences, supposed hidden meanings, patriarchal oppressions, deconstruction of texts, and multiple readings.

To Hazlitt this latter enterprise would have seemed mere

futile pedantry. Literature, theatre, art and philosophy were in his view matters of direct concern to the experience of life; they made a practical difference; therefore they were to be encountered and evaluated not only with discrimination and thought but with feeling – and honestly so.

Honesty is the key. Once can praise a book because one likes it, but one cannot dispraise it because one dislikes it – still less if, merely, one dislikes its author – unless one gives reasons, and makes a case for saying it is bad.

There are many ways that reviewing can be dishonest. Here is one illustration, drawn from no less a personage than the self-appointed doyen of the literature dons, Terry Eagleton. A standard rhetorical device in discursive literature has the form 'Some say X, but I say Y.' The author might not disagree with X, but thinks Y is the more important point. A scurrilous reviewer can systematically misrepresent the author by saying, 'the author says X' and omitting the author's rider 'Y'. This is one of Eagleton's techniques of choice (chapter and verse can be abundantly supplied). Of course, this might not be intentional on Eagleton's part; he might merely be stupid or lazy. But since it is better to doubt this, we have to conclude instead that he is guilty of wilful misrepresentation. It is alarming to think that such are the ethics of criticism he teaches his students at Manchester University.

Bad reviewing – the giving of bad reviews without a good case – is less usually the product of malice than of conceit. Young male reviewers new on the block, armed with more arrogance than experience and naked but for their wit, are apt to lay about them in an effort to be noticed. In one respect this is a good thing from the young man's own point of view, for it is useful to make enemies early in life, given that the best lessons come from bloody noses. Anyone who wishes to think clearly, judge soundly and write well is lucky, therefore, if he has a Meno moment at the commencement of his career. Meno, recall, was the insufferably cocky young Thessalian who thought he could teach Socrates what virtue is; and who learned that it was only by grasping the extent of his ignorance that he could begin to be wise.

From all points of view a book does best to get mixed reviews, for then the reviews do not stand in any reader's way, and – as Wilde remarked – the author can know what he most wants to know: that he has done something right.

Reading reviews is a pragmatic exercise for the majority of those who do it. Browsers of book pages can be turned into buyers by a reviewer's enthusiasm, which is often what readers themselves hope will happen. Writing reviews might also, for some, be a pragmatic exercise; in the past aspiring novelists eked a living thereby, though it is hard to see anyone doing it now. But for others it is a pleasure, even a passion and a delight. Part of the reason is that reviewing is highly educative. It makes one read far more, and far more widely, than is usual even among bibliophiles. And one does it with the special watchful intent required by the duty to engage and respond, to make a judgement and a case for that judgement.

There can be no better way to illustrate one form of the business of reviewing than by reviewing a couple of reviewers when they are themselves both doing and commenting upon the reviewing craft. I choose, respectively, Harold Bloom and his *How To Read and Why*, and Michael Hofmann and his *Behind the Lines*.

It is easy to mix metaphors about Harold Bloom. He is the doyen of traditionalist literary critics, a bastion against the intellectual corruptions of post-modern air-headedness in 'critical studies', a champion of literature for its intrinsic life-enhancing value, a lion-hearted eagle-eyed reader whose appetite for books is immense and admirable. He is all these things, and he is also a vastly over-prolific author and editor – hundreds of books are credited to him in one or the other capacity – who has said the same thing so often over so many years that he is like a mathematical fractal: any page written by him recapitulates all his other thousands.

The essence of Bloom's view is that Shakespeare and Cervantes are the two touchstones for almost everything in life, the universe, and literature; that Dr Johnson and William Hazlitt are the two greatest critics (perhaps we should add: before Bloom) of all three; and that irony is indispensable. These key concepts unlock the Bloom canon of thought, and are the endlessly iterated themes of this condescendingly-titled, peculiar, repetitive, fascinating, irritating, and ultimately enjoyable *How To Read and Why*, which – as suggested by Bloom's references to his age (seventy or thereabouts when he wrote it) – has something of a hurried valedictory air about it, as well as the feel of hastily scratched-together lecture notes and jottings. It glitters like a sequinned ball-gown with *aperçus* and insights, but among the paste and occasional false lustre of the costume jewellery there are diamonds. And sometimes Bloom is thunderously wrong – which is itself valuable, because he thereby ignites explosions of disagreement that prompt thought; and anyone who makes us think does us a service.

Why read? In Bloom's view we read for pleasure, for the companionship literature provides, and to 'strengthen the self' – a vague phrase denoting something like self-improvement. And he claims that the value of reading is 'selfish rather than social' because we can make only ourselves, not others, better by reading. This last point is one of his most egregious errors, for it entirely misses the fact that attentive and thoughtful reading educates and extends the moral imagination, giving us insights into – and therefore the chance to be more tolerant of – other lives, other ways, other choices, most of which we will never directly experience ourselves.

The 'how to read' part is more messy, because Bloom, like all literary critics, uses the term 'read' in an ambiguous way to mean more than just moving one's eyes along a printed line to absorb its sense. Indeed this innocuous-sounding procedure is impossible, according to the Lit. Crit. fraternity, for whom to read is to construct and interpret, to fill the text with the reader's own meanings. Authorial intentions, and the fact that language is a public instrument of communication by whose means people standardly succeed in understanding one another and books, is overlooked in this refined theory. Anyway: Bloom is sufficiently of his time to mean 'interpret and gloss' by 'read' – but at least he thinks there can be a common or shared reading of a text, and when he sets out to show us how to understand and appreciate Cervantes, Jane Austen or Hemingway, he premises just such possibilities of agreement. That is good; the currently fashionable alternative premise, viz. that there are as many versions of *Emma* as there are readers of it, is relativistic nonsense of the first water.

After introducing the Why and How, Bloom sets off in seven-league boots over the literature of eight languages, two continents, and several centuries, dispatching in a page or two (occasionally more) Cervantes, Turgenev, Dostoevsky, Shelley, Shakespeare, Stendhal, Jane Austen, Chekhov, Milton, Herman Melville, Ibsen, Wilde, Toni Morrison, Wordsworth, Proust, Whitman, Borges – to name but a few, for the list is long and eclectic, and in effect constitutes a What to Read too, although he could justly claim to have already told us this in his *Western Canon*. Oddly, he falls into the usual mistake of forgetting the essayists – his own justly beloved Hazlitt among them – who count among the chief ornaments of English and indeed world literature. He summarises plots, gives a quick 'reading' of central themes, then hurries on. This would be a dissatisfying process were it not for the sequins and occasional diamonds everywhere glistening, and the occasional outrageousness.

Here are some examples of the latter. Minor disagreement is prompted by Bloom's claim (concerning Hamlet) that bookish intellectuals are by nature extremely ambivalent. Bloom himself is no such thing: does he not own a mirror? Major disagreement is prompted by Bloom's astonishing assertion that one of the greatest moral philosophers in literature, Jane Austen, wrote with no intention of commenting upon or challenging the ethics of her times, and required of her heroines only 'minor adjustments' in order to be rewarded with the Darcies and Mr Knightleys who are a properly well-regulated young lady's due. If there is a better and deeper study of moral epistemology than the initial misperceptions and mortifying re-educations experienced by Elizabeth Bennett and Emma Woodhouse, I do not know where to find it.

Among the striking ideas that everywhere blossom in Bloom is his view that Shakespeare's imaginative resources 'transcend those of Yahweh, Jesus and Allah', and provide a grander alternative vision of human nature. He is right. He says that genuinely intelligent people do not think ideologically; right again. He argues that literature is a form of the good; right yet again. Shakespeare's characters change upon hearing themselves, Bloom observes, whereas Cervantes' characters do so upon hearing what others say. That is a fascinating contrast, and a powerful point to meditate. Bloom insists that we should read without ideological baggage, without 'cant' (the platitudinous pieties of a fashionable orthodoxy), but instead with an open mind and fresh responses. This is not a new point, but the times are such that it merits forceful iteration. It is what in his own practice strikes sparks of insight such as those just mentioned.

The book's worst fault is its repetitiveness, and the fact that Bloom does everything by reference to Shakespeare and Cervantes, which does not add to their stature (such giants need no heightening) but reduces everything else in their shadow. That is a mistake; the summit of Parnassus is not a peak but a plateau, and there is plenty of room there for varieties of literature evaluable and enjoyable on their own terms without having to be Shakespearian or 'Cervantine' in some aspect of their nature. But if one ignores the repetitions and discounts Bloom's obsessions, there is a great deal of profit and enjoyment to be had from his pages.

Michael Hofmann is as enthusiastic as Bloom, but less professorial; he is as perceptive in his own way as Bloom, though more impressionistic, as is natural to the journalism rather than the scholarship of literature. The pieces in his *Behind the Lines* smack richly of his relish in the reviewing task. It is unsurprising that he should enjoy himself so much, given the privilege of his life as a reviewer: he is paid to write about poetry, fiction, theatre, film and art, and he ranges eloquently over them all in both English and German. This is no mean attainment to add to his considerable distinction as a poet and translator.

Perhaps the fineness as well as gusto of Hofmann's critical eye arises from the dual perspective that domestication in two languages provides. If so, he has equipment other reviewers well might envy. For when most other reviewers comment on the qualities of Musil, or of Rilke or Trakl, they are doing so across a linguistic gulf. As a native reader of these writers – more to the point: as a translator who knows intimately the space between the gulf's shores – Hofmann is at home. Yet he shows the same assurance in his commentary on writing (including poetry) in English, for which a secure set of intuitions about the language and its variegated genius are needed.

Hofmann is very generous when his enthusiasm is engaged – he can hardly find words enough to express his admiration for Elizabeth Bishop, Ian Hamilton as poet, James Buchan – while yet being careful to give proper due where he is less enticed. This is an engaging quality in a reviewer, for in manifesting a willingness to be unreserved in praise but temperate in criticism it shows that the reviewer knows how much endeavour goes into writing, and how few rewards it usually gets.

This, together with the ebullience and verve of his style, makes Hofmann a highly attractive writer. An unfriendly eye would see the breadth of his range as evidence of superficiality, the customary failing of dilettante inexpertise. But this is to mistake an important point about professional reviewing, which is that the development of its required skills is invariably fostered by exercise in different spheres. Few writers cross with as much ease as Hofmann does from writing about an exhibition of Otto Dix's paintings to giving an assessment of Joseph Brodsky's poetry, and moving from there to dilate upon a Wim Wenders film. But the same confident and accurate voice speaks throughout, spreading enlightenment and generating enthusiasm on each topic touched.

The best characterisation of Hofmann's criticism is given by contrast with what he says of Ian Hamilton's reviewing. 'It seems to me,' Hofmann says of Hamilton, 'that he hardly ever steps out and says what he thinks, in the first person, in his own voice ... he is impersonal and multitudinous.' This is emphatically the opposite of Hofmann himself. He is a lively presence in his criticism, frank and autobiographical, happy to take risks in judgement, and somehow always cheerful in the process.

In applauding the likes of Musil, Joseph Roth and Bohumil Hrabal, Hofmann does the more insular among his English readers a service, for he thereby keeps attention focused on writers likely to be remembered when some at least among contemporarily fashionable Anglophone names are forgotten (Hofmann mentions these latter, directly or in passing; but you have to read somewhat between the lines). His transcontinental sensibility licenses him in doing so, to the benefit of readers of English; for his is the larger perspective that a view across the continent provides.

Biography

Biography broadens the vision and allows us to live a thousand lives in one.

ELBERT HUBBARD

Biography is a popular literary genre, and an important one. It is popular because it satisfies our profound interest in other people's lives, especially those made salient by achievement, accident, or celebrity. And it is important because insight into other lives is one of the chief materials we have for understanding our own: and sometimes for changing them in the light of the possibilities their differences from our own lives reveal.

The popularity of biography, always considerable, has increased greatly since biographers allowed themselves frankness in the handling of intimacies. That is a good thing: life is lived more behind drawn curtains than on public platforms, so to give a living sense of personal human history the biographer must lift veils. This satisfaction of our need to understand – something more exigent than mere prurience of curiosity – is what adds to biography's value.

There are many different kinds of good biography. No one technique, no one biographer, is uniquely good. Bad biographies are bad for the usual reasons that make books bad – poor writing, lack of insight, inadequate research, insufficient detachment or, alternatively, sympathy. For good examples of different kinds of good biography, by contrast, consider P. N. Furbank in his studies of Diderot and E. M. Forster, and Miranda Seymour portraying Ottoline Morrell, Robert Graves and Mary Shelley.

The late Francis Steegmuller was an idiosyncratic but masterly exponent of this intriguing art. He was the biographer royal to French culture, a literary-historical artist of subtle and engaging gifts, some of whose books are to biography what the Lloyd's Building is to architecture: essence turned inside out, showing the works on the surface, offering themselves as visible assemblages of what, in other biographers' hands, would be their most secret moving parts.

A good introduction to Steegmuller's method is his perfect miniature of the exquisite friendship between the Abbé Galliani and Madame d'Epinay. It immediately whets the appetite for *Flaubert and Madame Bovary*, his masterpiece. But to exemplify the sides, shapes and aspects of Steegmuller's understated genius, one might choose a slimmer volume, in which his technique appears in unselfconscious and therefore representative mode: his amusing, surprising, touching *Apollinaire*.

Guillaume Apollinaire – the flamboyant, revolutionary poet in the vanguard of literary and artistic Parisian life before the First World War, friend of Picasso, Braque, Derain and Cocteau, one of the founders of Cubism and coiner of the word 'Surrealism' – was born Wilhelm Vladimir Alexandre Apollinaris de Kostrowitski in 1880 at Rome. His mother was an unmarried Pole, all of whose lavish exoticism, sensual appetites and large Slavic bones Apollinaire inherited. His father, as unknown to his son as to history, might have been Italian. The multiple and itinerant nature of Apollinaire's origins inclined him to seek a centre, and a language, for the expression of his genius; he found both in Paris. The two volumes of verse that immortalised him were published there in 1913 and 1916, respectively *Alcools* and the revolutionary *Caligrammes*. He was awarded a Croix de Guerre upon being seriously wounded in the head near Verdun;

and as the huzzahs greeting news of Armistice rang under the windows of his apartment in November 1918, he fell victim to the terrible influenza epidemic then sweeping Europe, crying out to his doctor 'Save me! Save me! I have so much left to say!'

Steegmuller winds the thread of his account of Apollinaire onto the spindle of a central event: the poet's arrest in 1911 in connection with the theft of the *Mona Lisa* from the Louvre. It turned out that the poet was not the thief, nor, despite police suspicions, did he know the thief. But he had, to his own and Picasso's supreme discomfiture, been involved in a related matter. In 1907 an acquaintance, one Gery Pieret, had stolen two ancient Iberian stone heads from the Louvre and sold them to Picasso, who was much influenced by them: they prompted the first-ever Cubist painting, his *Demoiselles d'Avignon*. Pieret continued to filch portable antiquities from the Louvre, whose security was non-existent, until in 1911 he revealed the story to the *Paris-Journal*, at the same time returning some of his latest acquisitions to the Louvre via that newspaper. Because of the resulting brouhaha Picasso became exceedingly nervous about his Iberian heads, and plotted with Apollinaire to return or otherwise get rid of them. In a state of great anxiety the two decided to throw them into the Seine, and crept thither in the small hours of night, carrying the heads in a bag. But honour prevailed, and the next day Apollinaire took them to the *Paris-Journal*, requesting anonymity and explaining the circumstances.

The newspaper professed surprise when Apollinaire's identity became known to the police. He was arrested, and there followed a miserable experience of one night's incarceration and examination by a magistrate, which Apollinaire subsequently turned into journalism, indulging the mild temerity of calling his article 'My Prisons' after the celebrated book by Silvio Pellico describing years of hell in the grim dungeons of Spilberk in Moravia, with its precisely-engineered torture equipment and rats. But: to a man of grand imagination, a few hours in a cell come to the same thing.

The air of mystifier and prankster that clung round Apollinaire as a result of this and other events interfered with early reception of his poetry. Was it new art, people wondered, or another escapade or joke? Even as his literary stature grew in the eyes of successive generations, something of ambiguity lingered. It no longer does so: the evocative simplicity with which Apollinaire catches fragmentary, transient, supercharged moments of experience and feeling, all of them intimately autobiographical, is high art.

Steegmuller's technique of collage, quotation and embedding – in which he speaks of his own quest for Apollinaire, and his meetings with people who knew him – gives immediacy to the book's narrative thrust, and adds texture and depth. Very extensive quotation must, on the face of it, seem undesirable; but Steegmuller uses it consciously and creatively, to introduce variety in the narrative voice, and a sense of actuality. The Louvre drama, for example, is played out in Steegmuller's account through the newspaper reports of the day, which make thrilling reading.

Good biography leaves one with a sense of having actually encountered a person and an age. Every time one closes a Steegmuller book, the sense of both is vivid.

Becoming Philosophical

Philosophy begins in wonder. And, at the end, when philosophic thought has done its best, the wonder remains.
ALFRED NORTH WHITEHEAD

When asked my profession, I say that I teach philosophy. Sometimes, with equal accuracy, I say that I study philosophy. The form of words is carefully chosen; I do not say 'I am a philosopher,' for a certain temerity attaches to the claim – a claim which, because it seems to assert too much, does not sound as straightforwardly and unpretentiously descriptive as 'I am a barrister/soldier/carpenter.' The title of philosopher, especially as denoting Socrates, Aristotle, Descartes, Spinoza, Kant and other great thinkers in history, is an honorific which can only properly be applied by third parties and only to those who merit it. And such need not necessarily be – indeed, may well not be – academic teachers of the subject.

When I reply in the way described, I see further questions kindle in the interrogator's eye. 'What do philosophers do in the mornings when they get up?' they ask themselves, privately. Everyone knows what a barrister or carpenter does. The teaching part in 'teaching philosophy' is obvious enough; but the philosophy part? Do salaried philosophers arrange themselves into Rodinesque poses, and think – all day long?

But the question they actually ask is, 'How did you get into that line of work?' The answer is simple. Sometimes people choose their occupations, and sometimes they are chosen by them. People used to describe the latter as having a vocation, a notion borrowed from the idea of a summons to the religious life, and applied to medicine and teaching as well as to the life of the mind. No doubt there are people who make a conscious decision to devote themselves to philosophy rather than, say, tree surgery; but usually it is not an option. Like the impulse to write, paint, or make music, it is a kind of urgency, for it feels far too significant and interesting to take second place to anything else.

The world is, however, a pragmatic place, and the dreams and desires people have – to be professional sportsmen, or prima ballerinas, or prime ministers – tend to remain such unless the will and the opportunity are available to help them onward. Vocation provides the will; in the case of philosophy, opportunity takes the form of an invitation, and a granting of licence to take seriously the improbable path of writing and thinking as an entire way of life. In my case as for others, the invitation came from Socrates.

When Socrates returned to Athens from his military service at Potidiae, one of the first things he did was to enquire into what had been happening in philosophy while he was away, and whether any of the current crop of Athenian youths was distinguished for beauty, wisdom, or both. So Plato tells us at the beginning of his dialogue *Charmides*, named for the handsome youth who was then the centre of fashionable attention in Athens. Always interested in boys like Charmides, Socrates engaged him in conversation to find out whether he had the special attribute which is even greater than physical beauty – namely, a noble soul.

Socrates' conversation with Charmides was the trigger that made me a lifelong student of philosophy. I read that dialogue at the age of twelve in English translation – happily for me, it is one of Plato's early works, all of which are simple and accessible; and it immediately enticed me to read others. There was nothing especially precocious about this, for all children begin as philosophers, iterating their wonder at the world by means of the 'wh–' questions – why, what, which – until the irritation of parents, and the schoolroom's authority on the subject of Facts, put an end to their desire to ask them. In just that way I was filled with interest and curiosity, puzzlement and specu-lation, and wanted nothing more than to ask such questions and to seek answers to them forever. My good luck was to have Socrates show that one could do exactly that, as a thing not merely acceptable, but truly worthwhile, to devote one's life to. The nature and subject of the enquiries he undertook seemed to me the most important there could be. And I found his forensic method exhilarating – and often amusing, as when he exposes the intellectual chicanery of a pair of Sophists in the *Euthydemus*, and illustrates the right way to search for under-standing. Presented with such an example, and with such fas-cinating questions, it simply seemed obvious that no vocation could rival philosophy.

These juvenile interests were more or less successfully hidden from contemporaries in the usual way – under a mask of cricket, rugby, and kissing girls in the back row of the cinema – because being a swot was then as always a serious crime; but although all these disguises were agreeable in their own right, especially the last (the charms of Charmides notwithstanding), they could not erase what had taken hold underneath – a state of dazzle-ment before the power and beauty of ideas, and of being fas-cinated both by the past and the products of man's imagination. The fever never abated.

This youthful discovery of philosophy occurred in propitious circumstances, in the sense that I grew up in a remote region of the world, the parts of central and east Africa described by Laurens van der Post in his *Venture into the Interior*. This was before television reached those high dusty savannahs and stupendous rift valleys, and therefore members of the expatriate English community there, of which my family was part, were much thrown on their own devices, with reading as the chief alternative to golf, bridge and adultery. In the pounding heat of the African tropics all life is shifted back towards dawn and on past evening, leaving the middle of the day empty. School began at seven and ended at noon. Afternoons, before the thunderstorms broke – one could set the clocks by them – were utterly silent: almost everyone and everything fell asleep. Reading, and solitude of the kind that fills itself with contemplations and reveries, were my chief resources then, and became habitual.

With parents and siblings I lived the usual expatriate life of those distant regions before Harold Macmillan's 'winds of change'. It was a life of Edwardian-style magnificence, made easy by servants in crisp white uniforms, who stood at attention behind our wicker chairs when we took our ease on the terrace, or beside the swimming pool or tennis court, in our landscaped garden aflame with frangipani and canna lilies. Early reflection on this exploitative style of life, together with the realisation that Plato's politics are extremely disagreeable (today he would be a sort of utopian Fascist, and perhaps even worse), gave my political views their permanent list to port.

My mother always yearned for London, and clucked her tongue in dismay, as she read the tissue-paper airmail edition of *The Times*, over the shows and concerts being missed there. I agreed with her, in prospective fashion. But a good feature of this artificial exile was the local public library. It stood on the slope of a hill, on whose summit, thrillingly, lay the skeletal remains of a burned-out single-seater monoplane. In the wreckage of this aircraft I flew innumerable sorties above imagined fields of Kent, winning the Battle of Britain over again. But I did this only in the intervals of reading under a sun-filled window in the extraordinarily well-furnished little library, a paradise to me. I had the good fortune to meet Homer and Dante there, Plato and Shakespeare, Fielding and Jane Austen, Ovid and Milton, Dryden and Keats; and I met Montaigne on its shelves, Addison, Rousseau, Dr Johnson, Charles Lamb and William Hazlitt – and Hume, Mill, Marx and Russell. From that early date I learned the value of the essay, and fell in love with philosophy and history, and conceived a whimsical desire to know as much as could be known. Because of the miscellaneous and catholic nature of these passions, the books in the rich little library gave me a lucky education, teaching me much that filled me then and fills me still with pleasure and delight.

One aspect of this was the invitation to inhabit, in thought, the worlds of the past, not least classical antiquity. In ancient Greece the appreciation of beauty, the respect paid to reason and the life of reason, the freedom of thought and feeling, the absence of mysticism and false sentimentality, the humanism, pluralism and sanity of outlook, which is so distinctive of the cultivated classical mind, is a model for people who wish to believe, as the Greeks did, that the aim of life is to live nobly and richly in spirit. In Plato this ideal is encapsulated as *sophrosyne*, a word for which no single English expression gives an adequate rendering, although standardly translated as 'temperance', 'self-restraint' or 'wisdom'. In his most famous and widely-read dialogue, the *Republic*, Plato defines it as 'the agreement of the passions that Reason should rule'. If to this were added the thought – reflecting the better part of modern sensitivity – that the passions are nevertheless important, something like an ideal conception of human flourishing results.

When not in Athens I was in ancient Rome. For the Romans in their republican period something more Spartan than Athenian was admired, its virtues (*vir* is Latin for 'man') being the supposedly manly ones of courage, endurance and loyalty. There is a contrast here between civic and warrior values, but it is obvious enough that whereas one would wish the former to prevail, there are times when the latter are required, both for a society and for its individual members. For a society such values are important in times of danger, such as wartime; and for individuals they are important at moments of crisis, such as grief and pain. The models offered by Rome were Horatius – who defended the bridge against Tarquin the Proud and Lars Porsena – and Mucius Scaevola, who plunged his right hand into the flames to show that he would never betray Rome. Unsurprisingly, the dominating ethical outlook of educated Romans was Stoicism, the philosophy which taught fortitude, self-command, and courageous acceptance of whatever lies beyond one's control. The expressions 'stoical' and 'philosophical', to mean 'accepting' or 'resigned', derive from this tradition.

One Saturday afternoon when I was fourteen I bought – for sixpence, at a fête run by the Nyasaland Rotary Club – a battered copy of G. H. Lewes's *Biographical History of Philosophy*, which begins (as does the official history of philosophy) with Thales, and ends with Auguste Comte, who was Lewes's contemporary. Lewes was George Eliot's consort, a gifted intellectual journalist, whose biography of Goethe is still the best available, and whose history of philosophy is lucid, accurate and absorbing. I could not put it down on first reading, and in all must have read it a dozen times before feeling sated. It superinduced order on the random reading that had preceded it, and settled my vocation.

When I returned to England as a teenager it was to a place intensely familiar and luminous because whenever in my reading I was not either in the ancient world or somewhere else in history, I was there – and especially in London. Everywhere one goes in London, even on ordinary daily business, one encounters its past and its literature – retracing Henry James's first journeys through the crowded streets of what was in his day the largest and most astonishing city in the world, seeing

Dickens's Thames slide between its oily banks, and Thackeray's Becky tripping down Park Lane smiling to herself. Imagination supplied the roar from Bankside, whose pennants fluttered above the Bear-garden and the theatres, and displayed the crowds that milled under the lanterns of Vauxhall Gardens, where fashion and impropriety mingled. Deptford on the map seemed to me a horrifying name, because Marlowe was stabbed there. On the steps of St Paul's I thought of Leigh Hunt's description of the old cathedral, before the fire, when it was an open highway through which people rode their horses, in whose aisles and side-chapels prostitutes solicited and merchants met to broker stocks, and where friends called to one another above the sound of matins said or vespers sung. London is richly overlaid by all that has happened in it and been written about it. There is a character in Proust who is made to play in the Champs-Élysées as a boy, and hated it; he later wished he had been able to read about it first, so that he could relish its ghosts and meanings. Luckily for me I came prepared just so for London.

It seemed entirely appropriate to me later, as an undergraduate visiting London at every opportunity, to spend afternoons in the National Gallery and evenings in the theatre (every night if it could be afforded – and even when not) because that is what my companions – my friends on the printed page under the sunlit window in Africa, such as Hazlitt, Pater, and Wilde – intimated was the natural way of relishing life.

But it was not just the relish that mattered, for everything offered by art, theatre and books seemed rich grist for the philosophical mill – prompting questions, suggesting answers for debate and evaluation, throwing light on unexpected angles and surprising corners of the perennial problems of life and mind. An education as a philosopher involves studying the writings of the great dead, which enables one to advance to engagement with the technical and often abstruse debates of contemporary philosophy. But philosophical education requires more than this too, for in order to do justice to the question of how these debates relate to the world of lived experience – of how gnosis connects with praxis – a wide interest in history, culture and science becomes essential. The reason is well put by Miguel de Unamuno. 'If a philosopher is not a man,' he wrote, 'he is anything but a philosopher; he is above all a pedant, and a pedant is a caricature of a man.'

At Oxford I had the good fortune to be taught by A. J. Ayer, a gifted and lively teacher, and P. F. Strawson, one of the century's leading philosophical minds. There were other accomplished philosophers there whose lectures and classes I attended, but I benefited most from personal intercourse with these two. And when in my own turn I became a lecturer in philosophy, first at St Anne's College, Oxford and then at Birkbeck College, London, I appreciated the force of the saying *docendo disco* – 'by teaching I learn' – for the task of helping others grasp the point in philosophical debates has the salutary consequence of clarifying them for oneself.

Socrates liked to tease his interlocutors by saying that the only thing he knew was that he knew nothing. There is a deep insight in this, for the one thing that is more dangerous than true ignorance is the illusion of understanding. Such illusion abounds, and one of the first tasks of philosophy – as entertainingly demonstrated by Socrates in Plato's *Meno* – is to explore our claims to know things about ourselves and the world, and to expose them if they are false or muddled. It does so by beginning with the questions we ask, to make clear what we are asking; and even when answers remain elusive we at least grasp what it is that we do not know. That in itself is a gain. One of the most valuable things philosophy teaches is an appreciation of this fact.

Another is the permission to keep alive and fresh the child's curiosity which first prompts philosophy – and which first prompted me to take Plato's *Charmides* from the library shelf.

'Philosophy begins in wonder,' Alfred North Whitehead said, 'and when philosophic thought has done its best, the wonder remains.' Another thing Socrates could have said that he knew, because all students of philosophy know it, is that the wonder arrived at by philosophy is an enriched wonder, and one of the best possessions of the human spirit.

Philosophy

You cannot do without philosophy; for everything has its hidden meaning, which we must know.

MAXIM GORKY

Philosophy is a set of pursuits which, in various ways and across a range of endeavours, investigates truth, meaning, knowledge, reason, existence and value. These at first seem heady matters, but almost everyone at some time ponders them, so they are in fact familiar to everyone. The only difference between discussing them in a pub and studying them at university is that the latter endeavour aims to be more thorough and systematic.

Philosophy has always been concerned with two fundamental questions, one concerning the ultimate nature of reality, the other concerning its value. The questions are linked, in that they supply or at least suggest interpretations of each other. The second underlies all our debates about whether there is a transcendent source of value in the world, one that specifies goals for us and tells us how we must live and behave. Questions of God, morality and aesthetics lie under this heading, and even a negative answer – one that says there are no transcendent grounds of value, and that we must therefore find them within ourselves – is vitally important to us.

The first question might seem now to be the possession of philosophy's daughters, the natural sciences; but these latter in their own turn generate new forms of the ancient question, and so far have made slow progress with such puzzles as, for example, the nature of consciousness, and its role in shaping how the world appears to us. Questions about reality prompt crucial others about knowledge, truth and meaning – in short: the relation of mind to the world – and as with the question of value they invite us to seek not merely knowledge but understanding of everything comprehended under them.

These questions are examined, discussed, theorised about, and endlessly re-asked throughout human history, each generation making (and needing to make) its own attempt at answers. Philosophers debate with each other in depth, and often enough disagree; but the fact that there have always been more philosophers than schools of philosophy shows that they also often agree, with much of their debate co-operatively concerning minutiae and nuance.

Philosophical debates are also highly consequential, for philosophy is a productive enterprise. Consider what it has directly or indirectly given birth to in modern times: in the seventeenth century the natural sciences, in the eighteenth century psychology, in the nineteenth century sociology and empirical linguistics, in the twentieth century computing, artificial intelligence and cognitive science. Moreover, all the great debates in morality, religion, society and politics draw upon philosophy, and refer to it their conundrums and difficulties.

Isaiah Berlin said that the philosopher working in his study today can change the course of history within fifty years. He had in mind John Locke, whose writings were quoted verbatim in the documents of the American and French revolutions, and Karl Marx, whose name and ideas were bent to the purposes of Russian and Chinese revolutionaries in their respective endeavours. But he could as easily have cited the more diffuse and subtle ways in which movements of thought reconfigure the world, in the guise of belief systems, moralities, ideologies and intellectual fashions. Ideas are the cogs of history – and too often the barricades that stand in its way. Mankind is blessed with a creative talent for inventing and applying ideas, and cursed with an inability to shed them when their time is passed. No idea has been too bizarre to find advocates, and good sense has often seemed folly to those who cannot or will not think straight. For these reasons, ideas have been the most common source of conflicts in history.

One of the things philosophers like best about their job is that they have not just a right but a duty to stick their noses into all the world's intellectual affairs, from science to politics via art and everything else. If they bring to bear the ideals of their vocation – clarity, principle, insight and illumination – they do a service to mankind. And sometimes, as the progress of human knowledge shows, they even find answers to some of the endless questions they ask.

Reality

Our separate fictions add up to joint reality.

STANISLAW LEC

A major problem in trying to answer questions about the 'ultimate nature of reality' is the difficulty of settling a correlative question, viz. what is the relation between mind and the world? A contemporary illustration of what is at stake is afforded by quantum theory, the branch of physics which deals with the fundamental structure of matter. In this guise the question can usefully be cast as one about the relation between observers and what they observe. In the 1930s some physicists of the Copenhagen school argued that quantum theory forces us to think of reality as intimately related to observation of it. This theory is uncongenial to those 'realists' who, like Einstein, are committed to the classical view that reality is independent of any thought or experience of it.

The underlying dispute is an ancient one in philosophy, and it stems from a simple, obvious, but deeply puzzling fact: that one can by definition never observe an unobserved thing, and so can at best only guess what any unobserved thing is like. One cannot even claim with certainty that an unobserved thing exists. So any description one gives of a thing is a description of it as an observed thing. But to stand in the relation of observer to something is to interact with it. Might not interaction modify its character, perhaps drastically? It seems that we can never claim to know how anything is in itself, undisturbed by our relation to it.

According to the Copenhagen theory, observation does not merely interfere with reality but determines its fundamental nature. The phenomena only are what they are when we investigate them; beforehand there just is no answer to the question, 'What are things like?' This conclusion, that we cannot view the world as independent of our thought of it, is supported by another reflection: that we can never stand outside our minds to compare their contents with a putative non-mental realm which – so we suppose before we begin to think properly about it – our minds neutrally mirror.

The chief argument deployed by realists is that we should simply assume that the world is independent of us, because the best explanation of the coherence and regularity of our experience is to say that mind-independent entities, obeying physical laws, cause our experience by interacting with our sense-organs and scientific instruments.

To this plausible-sounding suggestion there are two objections. One is that even if we grant that this is indeed our best assumption, its being so does not guarantee its truth: an assumption can be the best available and still be false. And this prompts the second objection: that it is not the business of those who are investigating the nature of reality to assume anything about it in advance. In this field of enquiry we should not be making assumptions, but testing them vigorously.

Another suggestion advanced by realists is that independent reality is concealed from view behind a 'veil of ignorance'. Because our powers of enquiry are limited, they say, we find it hard, perhaps impossible, to penetrate the veil; but that does not entail that nothing lies beyond it.

To this move also there is an objection. If we say that there is an independent reality but it is inaccessible to us, we are asserting something which admits of no proof, as the claim itself states; and so the claim's net value is nil. Instead of solving our problem it merely restates it. At most we have simply turned a pre-scientific belief into an article of faith.

As these remarks are designed to suggest, the debate about how best to describe the relation between mind and the world is unresolved, and remains central to philosophy. Historical and contemporary efforts to proffer solutions are rich in fascinations and surprises.

The only consideration that could amount to a more tempting invitation to philosophy than this, is the promise philosophy also gives of materials for the considered life.

Values and Knowledge

The physicists have known sin; and this is a knowledge they cannot lose.

J. ROBERT OPPENHEIMER

One of philosophy's great endeavours is to understand reality; the other is to understand value, especially moral value. Here the central questions are: what are the best kinds of life for individuals, and which social arrangements would best allow individuals to construct such lives for themselves?

One aspect of these large questions is how education can assist in answering them; and a significant aspect of this aspect, in turn, is the particular question of how education can incorporate ways of promoting reflection on the ethical implications of our most powerful and successful way of knowing the world, namely, science; for the mastery given us by scientific knowledge prompts some of the sharpest ethical dilemmas faced by mankind. For just two of many examples, consider the enormous vistas of change opened for society by genetic engineering and embryo research. Some commentators argue that if our society is to engage in a thoughtful and responsible way with such challenges, it ought to ensure that study of them is included as a formal part of the science curriculum at schools and universities.

The point is a good one – but it is so good that it applies more generally than this formulation suggests. It is unquestionably right that education should promote reflection on ethical questions; but it should do so no matter what subject prompts them. There is in fact little in a standard school curriculum anywhere in the civilised world which fails to offer occasion for such debate. Literature, history, geography, the access to other cultures afforded by language study, even sport, can all provide materials for discussion of social and moral concerns. Science is not unique in presenting us with problems of value, and it is a mistake to think that studying (say) the Peasants' Revolt of 1381, or employment in the Sri Lankan tea industry, or Jane Austen's *Emma*, suggests fewer or less relevant ethical points than do recent advances in bioscience.

It is of course true that the speed and extent of science's progress make it urgent that people should consider what is and is not acceptable among its likely consequences. Responsible discussion of the astounding progress in genetics, for example, shows that it promises great rewards in medicine and agriculture, while at the same time forcing us to ask where it is leading human beings and the environment. Scientific ignorance on the one hand, and incompetence at ethical reflection on the other hand, are each capable of derailing the endeavour to reach sound decisions which take the best that science offers while protecting the best of what it might compromise. So, obviously, education in both is essential.

Still, the questions of value prompted by science are moral, not scientific, and are therefore entirely general. A rephrasing of the greatest such question is: what is valuable in the moral sense? A secondary question is: how can people be encouraged to live according to what is valuable? This latter question is as old as Plato; in his *Meno* he begins with it, in the form 'Is virtue teachable?', for it was then exercising the minds of upstanding Athenian citizens whose teenage sons were stealing chariots and being a nuisance. (There is, as the preacher in Ecclesiastes says, nothing new under the sun.) Socrates, in his wonted manner, claimed that he did not know the answer, on the grounds that he did not know the answer to the first and greater question, 'What is virtue?' This was his way of getting the debate going, for he indeed had answers to offer, but he only ever offered them when his opponents had fully appreciated the extent of their confusion – proving that confusion is the beginning of wisdom.

Most moralists, and certainly all those of a religious persuasion, think that pupils should be 'taught values' at school, not mainly so that they can apply them in thinking about the implications of science, history and other subjects, but to make them behave in ways that they (the moralists) find acceptable. But the point of equipping people to think about ethics is not to impose some partisan set of principles upon them, but to develop their powers of reflection, and to inform them of possibilities and options so that they can think for themselves.

There are nevertheless certain premises. Chief among the aims of an education in ethical reflection is to help people recognise and appreciate alternative points of view, to show why it is important to approach others in a spirit of respect, to demonstrate how essential it is to think about the consequences of one's own choices and actions, and to give an insight into the great possibilities that arise for people when their lives are lived in a setting of sympathy and tolerance. This is not prescriptive, but descriptive – for it draws on the experience of history to illustrate what conduces to human flourishing, and what militates against it. Such an education in ethical thinking would easily and well embrace all that science can either offer or threaten, as it embraces all that life itself can threaten and offer likewise.